In Praise of

"Through the use of personal stories and insightful conversations, Monica Hannan has opened for us a light into an often dark subject: death. With candor, humor and insights from experts and commoners, Monica has woven a masterpiece of cathartic analysis that undoubtedly benefitted her and her family, and all of us who have lost loved ones. Our last breath on the earth is followed immediately by our first breath in eternity – and for many the distance between those breaths is full of the unknown and uncertainty. Monica's compassionate work has made it less so."

--Kermit Culver
Senior Pastor, Legacy United Methodist Church

"High praise to Monica Hannan for exploring the taboo subject of death and dying through her observations, experiences, and messages of deep faith, hope, and trust. Hannan gives the reader permission to face the fears too often associated with death and offers a refreshing perspective - an understanding - that welcomes the rituals and comfort of letting go with love and dignity. Throughout *Gift of Death*, Monica Hannan beautifully weaves the personal journey of her father's death and reminds us that we all carry with us stories of death and dying that have significantly touched our lives. There is a universal connectivity in the "circle of life and death" that is revealed in Hannan's storytelling and readers may find themselves inspired to share their stories with loved ones. This work is an enlightening must-read for families of all faiths."

--Elizabeth Gross
Educator

"Monica Hannan's natural inclination to ask questions and seek information allows for many perspectives in this book. The stories shared, combined with her personal deep, faith-based beliefs bring a hopeful message about what is a difficult topic for many. This inspirational work reminds us, and helps us further understand, how we can truly enjoy life without trepidation over what's beyond."

> --Pete Miller
> Dreamer Ministries

"Monica Hannan has an inimitable way of blending accessibility and relevance – what folks would be interested in reading – with a kind of popular theological perspective which raises and probes important questions. As I made my way through the manuscript, it reminded me of so many occurrences and experiences in my own life and ministry, which is a signal to me that the book will be a true service to its readers."

> --Monsignor James P. Shea
> President, University of Mary

Gift of Death

A Message of Comfort and Hope

By

Monica Hannan

Semper Distinguit Publications

Dedication

To My Parents

Contents

Acknowledgments

I am essentially a private person. So, too, are many of the people who shared their highly personal stories, expertise, and insights with me. Without them, this book would not have been possible. To all of them I offer my deepest gratitude. You are a brave lot. I also wish to recognize my family, all of whom helped me in some concrete way to write these stories, and who gave of their time; Cliff, C.J., Meghanne and Hannah. I love you all and appreciate you all more than I can say. Thank you to all who read the manuscript in its various stages – especially Dick, Deb, Betts and Bonnie, Monsignors Richter, Lindemann, Schumacher, and Shea, Fr. Ehli and Bishop David Kagan. A special thank you to my editor, Betsy Sundquist and to my book designers, C.J. Naylor and Derek Milner.

Foreword

In a world of mysteries and wonders, the greatest mystery of all is death. Paul Gauguin painted a famous picture titled: "Where did we come from? What are we? Where are we going?" He borrowed the title from a Catholic catechism that posed these as the fundamental questions facing every human. Whatever our thoughts about life, whatever our likes and dislikes, whether we have been rich or poor, whether we have had an easy time or a life filled with anguish, we all come at last to the same end: death is waiting for everyone. "For of the wise man as of the fool," says the writer of Ecclesiastes, "there is no enduring remembrance, seeing that in the days to come all will have been long forgotten. How the wise man dies just like the fool! So I hated life, because what is done under the sun was grievous to me; for all is vanity and a striving after wind." In these melancholy verses can be heard the sigh of a race burdened by a shadow that it cannot evade or escape.

What then is to be done? How does one face the fact of death? Do we take the advice of the poet Dylan Thomas? "Do not go gentle into that good night. Rage, rage against the dying of the light!" Do we try to steal what satisfaction we can from our brief time among the living, as another poet has suggested? "Gather ye rosebuds while ye may, old time she is a-flying. And this same flower that smiles today, tomorrow will be dying." Or do we, as is fashionable now, just try not to think about death, behave as though it is not moving toward us, and remove it as much as possible from our sight?

The long Christian tradition has thought otherwise. "Remember death!" was the watchword of monks, not because they enjoyed dark and morbid thoughts, but because they knew that unless we can make sense of death, we can make no sense of life.

The great Christian epic recounts the tale of God himself, the Lord of Life, coming among us, taking on the burden of our death, wrestling that enemy to the ground, and defeating it. "Death, where is your sting?" was the triumphant song of the Christians, who, as the letter to the Hebrews puts it, had been delivered by Christ from lifelong bondage to fear of death.

This has meant that for believers death is no longer an insoluble mystery, nor a life-destroying tragedy. We can walk through death into life beyond the grave, following the path of death's destroyer. But if it is not a tragedy, death is still an ordeal. It involves a great change. It means the severing of all our ties of affection, at least temporarily. It means leaving behind all that we have known. It requires all the courage and wisdom and care that we can muster, for ourselves and for those loved ones near us who are facing imminent death.

This book by Monica Hannan treats the mystery of death in a lovely way, poignant and personal. Her aim is not a work of systematic theology, but a text which raises and probes important questions in a straightforward and accessible way. This is such good medicine for an age and a culture engaged in a futile attempt to dodge death, afflicted by a creeping despair that is all the more powerful because it is often unacknowledged. Monica beautifully helps her reader better to acknowledge the mystery of death so as to approach it anew. As I took to heart her insightful, experiential reflections, I kept thinking of the words of John Donne, who was able to write without flinching: "Death, be not proud, though some have called thee mighty and dreadful, for thou are not so;... One short sleep past, we wake eternally, and death shall be no more; Death, thou shalt die."

--Monsignor James P. Shea,
President, University of Mary

Introduction

I think most people are fascinated by the subject of death and dying. There have been many books written on the topic. For me, the question first came up because in my family, death was a taboo subject. Nobody ever talked about it. When somebody died we went to the funeral, we may have cried privately, but then we went on with our lives as if nothing had changed.

I gradually became aware of the reason. It was fear. Those closest to me feared death. I also had this natural fear, and because I believe in the power of information, I have always wanted to alleviate fear with facts: comforting information for myself and for those I love.

So I started asking questions. I went about it the way I have been trained, as a journalist. I have interviewed dozens of people on the topic, people of all faiths and backgrounds. I felt that others might benefit from what I found out, so I wrote this book. It is not about the near-death experience, although I will relate some of those events. It's about what happens in the moments leading up to death, both to the individual who is dying and to the family and friends left behind.

I will say up front that I come at this from a Catholic perspective. I was born and raised Catholic, I take great comfort from my faith and I needed to start somewhere, so this seemed a natural place to begin. However, I in no way believe that this information is strictly for people of a Catholic faith.

As a Catholic Christian, I believe in the power of Jesus to save, and I pin my hopes on that and simply trust that whatever happens after death will be good, not just for me, but for all who seek God with a sincere heart. What you will read in these pages is my certainty that as we approach death and prepare to meet God face to face, we will have the choice of whether to accept His grace. This is the free will He promised us. I am comforted by the knowledge that God loves us all and wants us all to be with Him, regardless of our religion or background, and yes, regardless of whether we believe in Him or not. Because God is love. The rest is up to us.

Monica Hannan

Chapter 1

If Death is a Part of Life, Why Do We Fear It?

I am not dying; I am entering into life. – St. Therese of Lisieux

My father's fear of death was like a living thing. It was the elephant in the room. We all knew it was there, but we pretended otherwise. If you brought it up, he'd look at you like you had committed some ghastly faux pas and change the subject. I believe his fear was so great that it kept him alive in situations that would have killed anybody else.

Born in rural Minnesota in 1930, he came from a staunchly Catholic family. There were two girls and five boys in his household, growing up together in a two-story farmhouse near Litchfield with uncles and aunts and a multitude of cousins living on surrounding farms. You might think their lives were idyllic, a sort of *Little House on the Prairie* existence, but those were hard times, and the family felt it. Surviving the Great Depression would have been difficult enough; add to that the fact that my grandfather suffered the curse of the Irish, the love of strong drink, and you have a recipe for some really lean years.

He was college educated, kind and honorable, but Grandpa was plagued by the tendency to binge drink. He didn't do it often, but when he went on a bender he could and did drink away all his money, then the family possessions, and eventually the farm. The family moved to California to start over when my father was in grade school.

In good times and bad, Sunday Mass was a given, even when my grandfather was at his worst. He was a deeply religious man with a strong belief in the faith of his childhood. God was real to him. He always tipped his hat when he passed a church, as if to say hello. His children attended Catholic schools, and the Hannan family could boast of one priest and several nuns. In fact, common lore of the day said that every Catholic mother should raise one child for the church. My father was the one my grandmother had her eye on.

It made sense that she would think this. During World War II, all of my father's brothers who were old enough served in various branches of the military. His brother, Robert, was a radioman in the Army Air Corps, and he and his crew were shot down over occupied Europe. He was declared missing, and for the entire year that my uncle spent hiding, once under a Dutch church altar, and often in partisan cellars and attics, my dad attended daily Mass to pray for his safe return. This did not escape the notice of his mother or the parish priest. One day Monsignor Moriarty and my grandmother pulled my father aside and talked with him about his obvious vocation. Shortly thereafter, he was enrolled in a nearby seminary. He wasn't there long. Devotion to God wasn't the problem; it was the prospect of celibacy. Dad knew fairly early that he wanted a traditional family life. His mother cried when he told her, and the priest sadly offered to pray for his soul.

After that, life at home was less attractive. His father's drinking led to frequent quarrels. His mother's unhappiness over that as well as Dad's decision to leave the seminary, and finally the fact that he simply didn't like being in school, caused him to drop out early, and at age 17 he joined the Merchant Marine. When the Korean Conflict broke out, he enlisted in the Navy, where he served on an aircraft carrier.

I asked him once whether he had ever been close to dying, and he said no and quickly dismissed the subject. But through careful questioning and close attention to the stories he told when his guard was down, I found out otherwise. There was the time he was strafed by a Russian MiG as he sat on the deck of the aircraft carrier, USS Essex. The buddy sitting beside him was cut in two by machine gun fire, but my father was untouched. He also contracted pneumonia during the war and had to be evacuated to a Navy hospital in Japan. He was so sick he remembered little about it, but he was told later that he had been very near death.

Another time, while hunting in the mountains of California, he was climbing up a cliff face on the edge of a ravine and he reached up to lay his rifle on the ledge above him, right onto a rattlesnake. It bit him twice in the hand. He showed me the scars. He was so far from medical care that by the time he reached the hospital, he was in critical condition and ended up in intensive care.

When I was eight years old, he was in an automobile accident that nearly killed him when he was thrown through the front windshield of his Volkswagen and into the fork of a tree. He suffered through prostate cancer, skin cancer, high blood pressure, heart arrhythmia and a leaky valve. He was obese, he smoked a pack a day for most of his adult life and he was a recovering alcoholic who spent the years between his early teens and his middle 50s drinking hard. Yet, through it all, he gave the impression that he would live forever. He worked as a security officer well into his 80s, quitting only after waking up one day face down in the parking lot after having suffered one of several heart attacks. At that point, it seemed a bad idea to be all alone in an empty building at night.

During the final year of his life, he suffered from congestive heart failure, an arthritic hip that never stopped aching, sciatica that sent shooting pains down his legs, a bone infection that caused him constant discomfort and steadily worsening weakness, yet he still talked about the future and what he would be doing next year and the year after that. In his mind, I don't think he could fathom what death would be like, and the unknown scared him, so dying simply wasn't an option.

Consequently, when I got the call that Dad was in critical condition and I should come right away, I was scared myself. It wasn't so much his dying that frightened me. It was watching *him* be frightened. I didn't feel that he was ready. What happened next changed my views about what it means to die.

Do not be afraid – Matthew 28:10

Fear of death is not unusual. In fact, it's the norm in American society. We don't want to think about it or talk about it. We've attempted to sanitize the entire thing. We're afraid to really look death in the face. In the United States, we've reacted to this fear by banishing death to institutions. Most of us will spend our final days in relative isolation in a nursing home or in a hospital bed connected to tubes and wires. In a sense, it seems that we are separated from the business of living long before we give up the ghost.

Monsignor James Shea, a Catholic priest and president of the University of Mary in Bismarck, North Dakota, attended seminary in Rome, Italy. There, he says they deal differently with death.

"Here in this country, there's a sort of scrubbed-clean character to the whole thing," he says. "What's happened is we've structured things, partly because of scientific progress that we've made. We've sort of programmed ourselves to think that all suffering is bad and we see death as a disease."

But in Rome, where he worked in a pediatric hospital, he says entire families come when a child is sick or dying, and they don't just visit, they essentially set up camp. "There was the sadness or grief that goes with a child dying, but there was a liveliness about it, too. Parents slept there, brothers and sisters were racing up and down the halls playing. There wasn't the solemnity that we tend to bring to it here."

In the Muslim tradition, families prepare their loved one's body for burial. They touch the body, clean it and wrap it in white fabric. They carry the body to the cemetery. Their personal involvement helps to bring closure in a way that sending flowers or a card, or even attending a funeral, may not. One medical professional whom I interviewed who is Muslim says the family lays the body in the grave, and those in attendance each throw in three handfuls of dirt. "You're reminded of where you come from and where you're going, as in your tradition, 'ashes to ashes, dust to dust.' And also, the bereaved family does not feel so alone."

He believes that the outward expression of grief that is so common in some cultures, but less so in the American culture, helps the person to heal faster. "People who cry seem to bounce back sooner," he says, but adds that the more sophisticated the culture, the less physical the expression of grief: "Those who don't express themselves are more likely to go into depression." He also believes that a closer involvement with the deceased person lessens a person's fear of death because they learn to see it as a natural part of life.

Shea says it's important to face death in order to see life as the gift that it is. And yet, it's also normal to be afraid. It's a built-in human reaction that is part of our will to survive. Plus, fear of the unknown resides in most of us. And of course, there is fear of pain. Even Jesus was afraid when He faced his own death. This is part of being human, just as it's natural to grieve for those we love even though we know their pain and suffering are at an end and our hope is that they are with God and we will eventually see them again. When you grieve, Shea tells me, God grieves with you, just as we feel the pain when our own children suffer.

Toward the end of his life, I gathered my courage and asked my father if he was afraid of dying and he said no, he'd lived a good life and was luckier than most, but I realized that was what he felt he *had* to say. To admit the fear out loud made it more real. We tell ourselves that everything will be fine, but there's another voice that most of us try not to hear – the voice of doubt.

Monsignor Tom Richter also trained in Rome, but now deals with death and dying as a matter of course as pastor of a large congregation. When a dying person tells him that he or she is afraid of death, he has a very straightforward answer.

"What is God like in a contrite person who is facing imminent death?" he asks them, then shares this thought: "God in a dying, contrite person is found in every thought, every feeling and every desire that is saying inside of that person, 'everything will be okay.' God wants us to feel comfort, hope, strength, faith. Those thoughts are from Him. The thing that isn't from God in those moments is fear."

He goes on to explain: "The great deceiver plants thoughts that get my focus on me -- my feelings, my regrets, my sins, and I get scared. I become focused on myself, trying to figure out what I need to do to make things right, when all I really need to do is trust in God.

"If you have been a bad man, what does God want from you at the moment of death? He wants you to have sorrow for sins, and if Catholic, to go to confession, certainly. But He also wants you to view Him as *Abba*. The enemy can attack a person at this time.

"Consider Judas. He saw what he did, and instead of being contrite and asking forgiveness and putting his trust in God as a father, he listened to his other voices and his betrayal overwhelmed him. What we need to do is trust that Christ will redeem us and we need to cling to Him."

He acknowledges that this can be difficult to do when you're sick and in pain. He says that's when those around you need to come forward and be your strength.

"You're on your deathbed, you're scared and discouraged. You think, 'Maybe God doesn't care. Maybe He's a fairy tale.' You start listening to the lie. But if there is someone in your room whose heart is in God, you can take your strength from that person. It's the job of the pastoral caregiver to quiet the lies that say, 'Heaven is not for you, that God doesn't care, that there is no Heaven.'"

Blessed too are the sorrowing; they shall be consoled – Matthew 5:4

Even for those who are convinced that there is life beyond this one, grief is part of the occasion. The dying grieve for those whom they are leaving behind, and for the pain that their loved ones are suffering, while the living grieve over the need to say goodbye. And this, too, is natural and God given.

"When Lazarus dies, why does Jesus weep?" asks Shea. "Even though Jesus knows He can fix the situation, He reacts to the grief of His friends. He takes in the sorrow of His friend dying. And remember, Lazarus did end up dying again. His return was temporary. The reason for Jesus' incarnation was to combat death. That was the whole purpose of His mission. Here's the great challenge for us, locked as we are in time and space. Tragedy brings our natural life to an end, and Jesus had that natural sense, too." But God is not bound by time and space.

"The spiritual world is the world we actually live in, we just can't see it," Shea continues. "We're stuck in the fog and we can't see beyond it. Death isn't traveling, it's awakening to what's all around us."

We have some knowledge of the next world from *The New Testament*. In Acts 7:55, we read of the martyr Stephen: *Stephen, meanwhile, filled with the Holy Spirit, looked to the sky above and saw the glory of God and Jesus standing at God's right hand.* St. Thomas Aquinas, one of the great writers of the Catholic Church, had a vision of Heaven as he was saying Mass that was so powerful, he stopped writing for good, describing his own efforts as no better than straw in comparison. And St. Paul, a man of words, said his visions of Heaven were so amazing that he couldn't even describe them.

In the modern era, St. Padre Pio, an Italian stigmatist and mystic who lived from 1887 to 1968, often spoke of Heaven as a place that we can't fully understand in our present state, although he received glimpses of it. He once said: "At night when I close my eyes the veil is lifted and I see paradise open up before me: and gladdened by this vision I sleep with a smile of sweet beatitude on my lips and a perfectly tranquil countenance." He also spoke extensively about his struggles with devils and agreed that both good and evil surround us: "The human soul is the battlefield between God and Satan."

Most of us can't see this battle being waged day to day, but somehow, at the moment of death, that wall between this world and the next can develop a crack that lets the dying peek in. Richter relates a story that many who deal with the dying have experienced.

"I was visiting a man in the hospital who was dying at night of cancer. He'd been sick for a long time and it was clear he wouldn't live much longer. He was struggling to breathe. As we gathered around him and I said the prayers for the dying, the Prayer of Commendation, I started saying the words, 'Go forth from this world.' At that moment his breathing, which had been strained, suddenly relaxed. A presence entered the room, and everybody in the room was aware of it. There were six or eight people there and we all became silent and just looked at each other. We all felt Him. The man breathed a few more times and then he died. People at that moment started praying spontaneously, things like, 'Thank you, Jesus. We love you, Jesus.' Then the family members started hugging and crying tears of wonder and gratitude to have been a part of it.

"I've had the same experience another time in the ICU saying the prayers for the dying. When I got to that particular moment in the prayers, the monitors went flat and everybody in the room felt the presence of God. That's not to say He isn't there if we don't feel Him, but this was a gift to those people."

Karen Hefner tells of her mother, Winifred Roberts, who, at the age of 88, had spent years basically bedridden after a series of strokes. She was cared for with great devotion by her husband for all 17 years of her illness, even after confusion began to overtake her and dementia robbed her of her ability to speak. He'd get her up into a chair every day, dress her, comb her hair, feed her. But one day she refused to eat.

"My dad was not going to just let it end," says Karen. As her mother became dehydrated, her father began frantically calling all over town, looking for someone who could start an IV to get fluids into her. He finally found someone who specialized in starting IVs in tough cases, and the man came to the house. Every time he'd get a line started, the vein would collapse. "He finally took my father aside and told him, 'If I didn't know better, I'd say she's collapsing her veins herself.'" Karen's father refused to give up, though. When the line was finally in, he sat up with her all night, holding her arm steady so that the IV wouldn't slip out. "It was almost as if she decided, okay, I'll keep trying for you," says Karen. Winifred started eating again. But two months later she slipped into an irreversible decline.

"She was sitting in the chair non-responsive, but she still made her feelings known. She would just turn her head when you tried to get her to eat. I tried to give her some juice and she refused that, too. I told my dad, 'She's done. She wants to go.' His response was, 'She can't be.' I told him, 'She's staying here for you. She tried to leave two months ago but now she can't do this anymore. You have to tell her it's okay.' But he couldn't do it. So I asked him if it was okay if I told her, and he said yes." They put her to bed and Karen climbed in beside her mother, lay close, put her mouth up to her ear, and whispered, "Mom, it's okay to go. We'll take care of Dad. I promise."

"Mom opened her eyes, sat up in bed, looked right into my eyes, then lay back down and relaxed," Karen says. Over the course of the next day and a half, life slowly ebbed from Winifred. "During that time she kept reaching out her arm, reaching up toward something or someone," Karen says. The family gathered around her, reading Psalms to her, just spending time with her and with each other through the night. In the morning, they left to go to breakfast, but Karen stayed. She was in the kitchen making herself a cup of tea when she noticed that nobody had taken her mother's vital signs that morning as they usually did, so she decided to do it. She went into the bedroom and took her mother's blood pressure first. It registered as "error," so she tried it again, with the same result. She took her stethoscope and listened and immediately heard her mother's heartbeat, but just once. After an entire minute, it beat again. At that point she woke her father, who was sleeping beside the bed, and told him that Winifred was going.

"He picked her up and held her in his arms and rocked her and cried. I just looked up and said, 'Into Your hands I commend her spirit,' and she was gone."

Karen felt peace at that moment along with her grief, then remembered a dream that she'd had days earlier.

"I was in the garden, just me and Dad and Mom. My mother was lying lifeless there and my dad looked up to heaven when she left, while I was the emotional one. We kind of reversed roles. But it was the same, just the three of us rather than the whole family around." She believes that was God's way of preparing her for what was about to happen. After her mother's death, she also had what she assumed were dreams in which she had trouble telling whether she was asleep or awake. "She was there. I'd feel her. Once, I was standing in my bedroom and I could feel her standing beside me." Finally she had a dream where her mother came and spoke to her. "She hadn't spoken in a long time, so it was wonderful to hear her voice. She was telling me goodbye and it was so peaceful and felt so real, but my husband, Curt, woke me up because I was crying. I remember being so mad at him because he woke me. But it was still a tremendous comfort." It is this comfort that God wants for each of us.

I will turn their mourning into joy, I will console and gladden them after their sorrows. Jeremiah 31:13

Chapter 2

Choosing the Moment

We are afraid of God's surprises! He always surprises us! - Pope Francis

People are fragile. Modern medicine has allowed many of us living in the First World to wrap ourselves in a cocoon of belief in the absolute wonders of antibiotics and emergency surgery. We fully expect to live to a ripe old age bolstered by medical science, and when we don't, we feel betrayed. Most of us don't have to deal with death on a daily basis the way our ancestors did.

Two hundred years ago, mothers gave birth to many children in the hope that at least a few would survive to adulthood. Often, couples didn't even name their babies until they got to their second birthdays, a time when the child was proven robust enough to have made it through the myriad of illnesses that killed infants before the age of antibiotics and vaccines. During just four years in the 1300s, plague wiped out nearly half of the population of Europe. Between 1918 and 1919, Spanish flu killed more people worldwide in a single year than the number who died in the four years of the

Black Death combined – somewhere between 20 million and 40 million people. But we aren't immune today. In the modern era, AIDS has killed more than 20 million people. And super bugs have become a significant threat, though the numbers are so far relatively small in comparison. We tell ourselves that we aren't in high-risk groups and therefore we're safe, but the reality is that a pandemic could strike again, and in fact, scientists tell us it's a matter of when, not if.

Still, most of us expect to live to a relatively advanced age, and most of us die of modern living, things like heart disease and cancer, relatively slowly. In other words, we have time to think about it, perhaps plan for it. Jesus told us that we know not the day nor the hour that the end will come (Matthew 25:13), but we push it to the backs of our minds. We don't dwell. Bring up the subject of death in a crowded room, and it brings the conversation to a standstill. But that's only at first. I have found that once a story is shared, people open up and want to tell of their own experiences dealing with someone who has died. It usually goes something like this:

"So you're writing another book?"

"Yes."

"What's it about?"

"It's about death and what happens to people as they approach death."

I'll get a blank stare back, then perhaps a nervous laugh. "Morbid," they might mutter and shrug their shoulders uncomfortably.

But then they think about it. And they'll ask, "So what have you found out?" Once the discussion begins, almost inevitably I find that they want to share a story that often they have never talked about.

This happened to me at a seminar for journalists over dinner in a restaurant. The conversation went along the predictable path, and then Dan Delgado, a longtime news manager, told me the following story.

Josephina Delgado, Dan's mother, was plagued by stomach pain for many months. She visited her doctor over and over, and he would prescribe antacids and send her home. After a while she was embarrassed to mention it because her doctor seemed to imply that it was all in her head or that she was overreacting to what was clearly indigestion. She came from a culture where women didn't want to make waves, so she kept her ever-increasing discomfort to herself. Only when it became impossible to ignore did she finally return to the clinic, where a specialist diagnosed her with stage four stomach cancer. Her doctors attempted surgery, but by then the cancer had spread throughout her body and there was little they could do. She was only 62 years old.

In the months leading up to Christmas, Josephina deteriorated rapidly. Her husband had to carry her to the car for her medical appointments; she became bedridden and soon lost the ability to care for herself, and finally could barely even talk.

On Christmas morning, four of her five children were visiting. They woke to the smell of breakfast cooking -- the traditional kind that their mother had always made. Before they knew what was happening, they heard Josephina's voice calling down the hall for them to get up because breakfast was ready. They were astonished to see their mother, who just the day before had been unable to rise from her bed or even talk, standing at the stove ready to serve. She remained with her children all that day, cooking, laughing and talking. They thought there had been a miracle, that she was suddenly on the road to recovery and that life would return to normal. They went to bed that night jubilant. But when they woke in the morning, Josephina was once again bedridden and unable to speak. She died a short time later. How can you explain that 16-hour miracle as anything other than a gift from God and a testament to a mother's extreme love?

This day you will be with me in paradise – Luke 23:43

People can and often do choose their moment of death, as perhaps Winifred Roberts and Josephina Delgado did. Hospice workers see this over and over again -- people who hang on just long enough for someone special to be there, or people who wait for special occasions or anniversaries. And sometimes they simply need reassurance that those they love will be all right when they go.

My friend, Jerry, was one of those people. He spent the last year of his life wasting away from cirrhosis of the liver and pancreatic cancer. When he finally reached the point where the hospital could do nothing more for him, his medical team began talking about hospice, but Jerry didn't want to go.

"He knew that once he made that trip, he was actually going to die," says his brother, Barry. "I hadn't seen him in a while and when I got the call to come, that he was dying, I didn't recognize him. He looked like a ghost, or a skeleton covered by skin. The only thing you could recognize were his eyes. I knew he wouldn't live much longer. You could see it just by looking at him.

"He was so worried about his wife and the kids, and how they would get along without him. The hospital staff told him that they were preparing to have him transferred by ambulance to the nearby hospice, but he kept saying no, he wouldn't go. I finally told him I was going to rent a limousine and that we would drive him any place he wanted to go, and do anything he wanted to do, but at the end of it, we would go to the hospice."

And that's what they did. During the ride, Jerry asked the driver to open the sunroof. As he looked out, he described the colors he was seeing as incredibly sharp. He described the trees as beautiful, almost fluorescent. Jerry was a photographer and he told his brother that the depth of field went on forever. "We drove around for a long time and it was quiet and weirdly calm. Nobody felt the need to talk. And finally he nodded that he was ready, and we took him to hospice."

When they arrived, there was an initial assessment, and a few short minutes later, as the family was busy filling out the admissions paperwork, a member of the staff told them that they should come to see Jerry right away.

"They told us if you want to talk to him, do it now, because he's ready to go. When we got to his room, his eyes were closed. I was holding one of his hands and his wife was holding his other. He couldn't talk at this point. I told him everything was okay and not to worry, that I would take care of Debbie and the kids. A single tear rolled out of his right eye and down his face. Debbie wiped it away, and at that moment he flat-lined. He was gone." Barry believes that Jerry held on until he was convinced that his family would be okay, but that once he'd made the decision, there was no longer any reason to linger.

The Lord God will wipe away the tears from all faces – Isaiah, 25:8

The Rev. Lori Lundblad is a hospice chaplain. She says it's not always the patient who resists hospice care; sometimes it's a family member who can't say yes to hospice because it feels like they're giving up on the person they love. And there can be misconceptions about what hospice is.

"Some people have this belief that when a loved one enters hospice, we're letting them starve," she says. "What's really happening is quite different, although it could look that way. Sometimes when the body is shutting down, it can no longer tolerate food or even water, and we have to explain to the family what's going on. Once they understand the process, it helps them to accept it."

The desire of the dying to take care of loved ones is a common theme that hospice workers hear. They tell story after story of people who hang on to life, waiting for reassurance, and sometimes they know more than the doctors do.

Bill and Ida Seuss were one such couple. Ida was very set in her ways and seemed to know every move that her husband would make. They began their married life on a farm in the town of Krem, North Dakota, a place that no longer exists. For more than 50 years, she made him the center of her world. She had her routines and she stuck to them without fail. Monday was wash day, Tuesday was baking day, etc. Breakfast was at 6, lunch at noon, supper at 5:30. It never varied, right down to the placement of the knives and forks on the table. Bill was more flexible. In fact, his grandson told me that he used a certain spoon for his coffee, one that Ida always laid out for him. He would drive her crazy with that spoon because he was always setting it down in a different place – the wrong place. Ida never failed to point it out, and then would return it to the place she considered proper.

Ida died on a Friday, with no warning. She hadn't been ill and, as far as Bill knew, the Thursday before had been like any other day. He woke up that Friday morning to discover that Ida had passed away in her sleep. Bill contacted his daughter and the family rushed over, but there was nothing to be done for her. It was only after the ambulance had come and gone, and after they started making plans for the funeral, that Bill realized that Ida had varied her Monday wash day routine, probably for the first time in their married life. The day before her death, on a Thursday, not her regular wash day, she had done the laundry, ironed his shirts, prepared his best suit and laid out his dress shoes. When he went into the kitchen, he discovered that she had laid out his cup and saucer for his morning coffee. But one thing was missing. The coffee spoon that he always used was not where she always put it. Instead, he found it where *he* always left it, in the place that drove Ida crazy. It was then that Bill realized that she must have had some sort of premonition, and that her last thoughts and actions on earth had been for love of him.

Woman, you have great faith! Your wish will come to pass – Matthew 15:28

The love we hold for others can be a powerful motivator. Debbie Roper was just pregnant with her fourth child when she felt a lump in her breast. She didn't tell her doctor about it right away because she believed it was cancer and if he knew, he would advise her to abort the baby, something that she wasn't willing to do. When she finally did tell him several months later, the tumor had grown to cover half her breast and was advancing aggressively. Her friend, Karen, says that toward the end, doctors kept testing her amniotic fluid to see if the baby was ready for delivery because they wanted to begin treatment as soon as possible to try to save Debbie's life.

"By the time the baby was delivered, a little girl they named Jessica, the cancer had spread into her lymph system and had metastasized to her hip," Karen says. "The surgeon who removed her breast gave her 18 months to live, at best." As Debbie held her newborn in her arms, she vowed to live as long a she possibly could for this child. She had three boys already, but they were older, and this was her first and much-longed-for baby girl.

"She wanted to raise her, so she asked God to give her 14 years," says Karen. "She thought her daughter needed her most until then." She began aggressive chemotherapy and radiation therapy, but her blood work still indicated cancer. Because she was sick and needed help with the children and her newborn, the family moved to Florida, where they could get the assistance of extended family. After she arrived, she made an appointment at a hospital there, where she had more X-rays and still more blood work. The treatments did not appear to be working and she was called to another appointment, this time to discuss last-ditch efforts.

"At that appointment they did her routine blood tests and X-rays," says Karen, "and she was sitting in the waiting room for her turn to see the doctor when a nurse came out and said, 'We need you to come back to the lab. We need to repeat the tests.' Of course, she assumed that the news was even worse than she'd anticipated, that perhaps the cancer had spread further." Again she sat in the waiting room, and suddenly she heard cheering coming from behind the nurses' station. "They called her back and the oncologist told her that not only could they not find the tumor, but her blood was clear of disease, and there wasn't even scarring at the tumor site. In essence, they told her there was no evidence that she'd ever had cancer at all." It appeared to be a miracle.

Debbie went back to her busy life as a mother, and the years flew by. When Jessica turned 14, Debbie went in for a routine visit, only to be told that the cancer had returned to the same spot in her hip, and this time it had come back with a vengeance. She died in her husband's arms a year later.

She had a special message for Karen in her final hours. "We had talked a lot about death," Karen says, "and I told her that I wasn't afraid to die, but I was afraid of *how* I would die and the pain involved. She told me, 'Don't be afraid. There's nothing to fear because God will be with you every step of the way.' It was a thing she really wanted me to know, and it brought me such peace."

People can and do make their own decisions about when it's time to release their hold on life. Dr. Dave Gayton, an emergency physician, gets a smile on his face when he talks about his grandmother.

"She was the kind of grandmother everybody would want to have," he says. She grew up on the Standing Rock Reservation, and "she was a wild child as a kid," he says. "She never lost that. She'd be out playing ball with us well into her old age, always playing with us. That's the kind of person she was, and she was also very independent. Her biggest fear, like a lot of people of her era, was ending up in a nursing home.

"She came into the ER one day and I happened to be working. By now she was in her 80s and prior to this still active and still living alone. But she was just not herself. She just kind of laid there, which was totally out of character. I didn't find anything specifically wrong with her, but you could see that she was failing." For the first time, he brought up the subject of a nursing home because she lived alone, and he was surprised when she agreed to go. She didn't put up much of a fight at all. In the interim, while arrangements were made, he asked her what she wanted to do: stay at the hospital or go home.

"She wanted to go home," he says. But she wasn't there long. "She knew she wasn't supposed to go up and down the basement stairs, and there was no reason for her to go down into the basement," he says. "But when we found her she was lying at the top of the stairs." She had died within hours of being discharged. "I can't prove it, but I believe she was going up and down the stairs. She was choosing her moment of death, and she wanted to die at home, not the nursing home."

Gayton didn't feel bad about the decision to let her go home, even though she died. "So often patients feel they're being dictated to," he says. "I let people in on the decision of what to do. This was what she wanted. She made her choice about how she wanted to die."

What his grandmother understood was that death is a journey, and she was ready to take the next step.

Chapter 3

Stepping Through the Door of Death into Eternal Life

God sustains every creature at every moment of our lives. He holds us in being. If he takes his attention from you, you'd cease to exist. God is love, and love is the only thing sustaining our existence. – Msgr. James Shea

We talk often about the moment of death, and while some of us may die instantly as in a car crash, for most, dying is a process that can take hours or days, especially if there has been a long illness.

When a person's heartbeat and breathing stop, it's called clinical death. Biological death happens four to six minutes later, when the brain cells begin to die from lack of oxygen. This is why those who work closely with the dying, such as hospice workers, will often tell family members that the patient can still hear them even after breathing has stopped. It may also explain the near-death experience, when people hover between this world and the next. What we do know from those experiences is that death itself does not seem to be a scary experience once it starts. Most people will describe a feeling of peace and joy, and if they come back from the experience, they've lost their fear of death.

In my first book, *The Dream Maker,* I describe in detail missionary Patrick Atkinson's near-death experience during adolescence that changed the course of his life. It was peaceful, there was a quick life review and he had the classic experience of traveling through a long tunnel toward an all-encompassing light, seeing people waiting for him as through mist, a feeling of joy and then being asked to return to his body because he had more to do in his lifetime. The encounter with life on the other side eliminated his fear of death, allowing him to do necessary work for the poor that at times has been very dangerous. If we all had that opportunity to die and come back, he believes that it would undoubtedly go a long way toward easing our fears.

"Everybody I know, without exception, who has had a real near-death experience comes out completely convinced of an afterlife and of the existence of God," he says, "although their concept of what or who God is may be different, depending on their perspective. A Hindu's impression of a near-death experience is not of the Christian God; it's unique to their faith, but that's to be expected because God is the God of many faiths." Atkinson finds that those who have the experience don't need to convince others that it happened or even explain it. It's just an absolute awareness that this life is not all there is. "What they lose is that natural fear of death," he says. But relatively few of us are afforded that opportunity.

Oh death, where is your sting? – 1 Corinthians 15:55

Much more frightening than death, to some, is the prospect of living connected to machines with little hope of returning to a meaningful life, as often happens in our final illness. It's especially true in the case of the elderly. In his work in the ER, Gayton has been at the bedsides of hundreds of dying people. He says those experiences have convinced him that death itself is not frightening. He believes we fear it because we don't see it very often as people live longer. Unless we're felled unexpectedly by accident or sudden illness, most of us will die in the hospital rather than in our own beds, typically of wasting illnesses that accompany old age.

Gayton also grew up on the Standing Rock Reservation, where the average life expectancy for a man is half what it is for the average American male. Perhaps because death happens so often there, he says the entire experience is different.

"When somebody is in the emergency room and they're dying, it's typical for very close family to be around them, but if it's a Native American person, 40 or 50 people will show up. A crowd gathers. And it's not just blood relatives. Their idea of extended family is stronger. When a person on Standing Rock dies, they don't hold the funeral in the church, they hold it in the school gym because so many people show up. When you experience that many deaths, it tends to ground you."

Gayton says he has discussed death with colleagues in the ER, and they tend to agree on one thing. They don't want to be kept alive artificially once their ability to live a fruitful life is behind them. They don't want extraordinary measures taken. They have seen enough pain and suffering to know that when it's their time, they are okay with dying and moving on.

"A lot of people who come into the ER say they want everything done," Gayton says. Sometimes it's their own fear of dying that motivates them. But often, it's because they don't want to let their families down, or, as in the case of Jerry, they worry that family won't be taken care of once they're gone.

Gayton says it's often part of his job to have a heart-to-heart discussion with patients and families about what "do everything to save them" really means. There are different levels of care in a hospital, and if the patient hasn't expressed his or her wishes clearly, it can come down to a decision by family members. That's why he says it's important to have these discussions before the need arises, because it can be very stressful and burdensome on families when they don't know what the dying person would have wanted once he loses the ability to speak for himself. Gayton often must discuss the levels of care for the dying with family, although he prefers to have the conversation directly with the patient when possible.

"Basically, when somebody dies it's because their organs start to fail," explains Gayton. This can be sudden or happen over a prolonged period of time. These organ failures can impact the central nervous system, the circulatory system, the kidneys or liver, or the respiratory system. A patient who is facing sudden death may be in shock. All of these things eventually happen when death is imminent. This is all part of the discussion of what life support will mean.

"Code 1 means you do whatever you have at your disposal to keep someone alive," Gayton says. This typically begins with measures that the hospital takes to make sure that the patient keeps breathing, or the ABCs of resuscitation. This involves keeping the airway clear and keeping oxygen flowing in and out of the lungs, typically by inserting an endotracheal tube and attaching it to a ventilator. And finally, circulation of blood throughout the body is typically supported through intravenous fluids and medications. These are measures taken to support failing organs. When you see a patient in the ICU attached to tubes and wires, all of this together makes up what we commonly call life support. If a patient is at the end of life and there is very little chance that they'll ever recover these bodily functions without the aid of machines, Gayton says it's important that patients and families understand this. "Once they do," he says, "most will say 'no' to Code 1 care."

Code 2 is what many people choose, when there is still hope of recovery to a level where the individual can function without life-supporting machines. "This means you treat the illness, but if it comes down to it, no life support is offered," he says. This is often what people mean when they say they don't want extraordinary measures. It does not mean withholding water or nutrition when it's possible to provide those.

And finally there is Code 3, often called palliative or comfort care. With this kind of care, the patient is kept as comfortable as possible, and the dying process is allowed to occur naturally, however long it takes. Most of the time, patients can receive enough medication that they are not in pain or distress as their bodies begin to shut down.

Once I was dead, but now I live forever and ever - Revelation 1:17

Families want to give their loved ones every chance at survival, particularly if the patient is young. But when you think about it, God certainly has a say in when your life on earth should end, regardless of the measures taken to keep you here.

Scott McFall was born three months early and with a faulty heart. By every medical measure, he should be dead. As he describes it, he's gone through his whole life with near-death happening redundantly, beginning in childhood. But his most life-changing series of events happened about eight years ago at the age of 39, when he went in for a routine physical and was told that his aorta was four times the size it should be, and he needed emergency surgery to repair it.

"It was the kind of surgery where they stop your heart and put everything on ice," he says. Afterward, in the ICU, his heart stopped repeatedly over the course of several hours. "I was being shocked back and then dying, shocked back and then dying," he says. Doctors put in a pacemaker that kept firing, and his heart wouldn't maintain a normal rhythm. "My family was told at one point that I was dead," he says. He doesn't know why he's still here, but he does know that his life was changed by the experience of dying over and over again. He says his near-deaths gave him insight at the time, although he didn't necessarily take what he learned and immediately put it to good use. He says instead that he "went into a self-indulgent digression" for a while. The trauma of it affected not just him, but those around him. "It didn't just change me," he says. "It changed the way the people around me behaved. There are people who react to the trauma of someone nearly dying by wishing that the person actually *had* died, even though they realize that's not rational. The stress of worrying that they'll have to go through it all again makes them behave differently toward you. And in the end they may leave."

McFall went into the physical believing that he was healthy. He was running every day and going to the gym, and when he came out of the surgery he was very, very sick. He couldn't walk. He'd had the circulation to his brain interrupted over and over again, so there was a question as to whether he had permanent brain damage and whether he'd spend the rest of his life in what he calls "a diminished capacity."

"I wasn't the same person and some people around me found that difficult to deal with," he says.

Plus, while he was in the ICU and those closest to him expected him to die, they talked to him in a way they might not have had they known he could hear every word.

"When I came out of anesthesia, I was on a respirator and I had extreme consciousness," he says. "I was very lucid. The issue was, people didn't know what I could or couldn't hear, so they started spilling their guts to me, or talked about how they were dealing with things. Here I was, not sure I'd even live, and I was in the bizarre position of feeling like I needed to comfort *them* or make the situation less stressful for them. It was fascinating, but it did change those relationships." Because of that experience, he believes that dying can be a very lonely process. He says the very young and the very old said wonderful things, but others tended to be focused on themselves.

McFall still lives with the knowledge that he could die at any time, but he says it's okay because his experiences have left him with an absolute assurance that life does not end when we die, because even when his body had stopped functioning, his consciousness, his thoughts, his awareness, all of those things that make him *him,* were still there. "My consciousness existed elsewhere, not in my body. I existed somewhere else. I was very aware."

Gayton says every death is different and as with Scott McFall, sometimes surprising things do happen. "You see people come in and you think, 'No way can they survive,' yet they do. Others come in and you think they're going to be fine and pull through who fool you and suddenly die." And very often the patient has some say in what the outcome will be, through sheer force of will.

Give some evidence that you mean to reform - Luke 3:8

Sometimes it's regret that can make the end of life painful, and it's during those times that you need the strength of others.

Father Ronald Giannone is a Capuchin friar who for most of his career worked with the Ministry of Caring in Wilmington, Delaware, devoting himself specifically to the care of people dying of AIDS. He says death should be a joyful experience because it's the moment when you meet God face to face and your existence becomes what God intended it to be. It should be a liberation. Yet people can bring unresolved issues to it that cause them pain and anxiety. "If you live in anxiety, you die a thousand deaths," he says. "Being able to discuss matters openly is much better." Particularly painful to see, he notes, is people who are estranged from their families because of life choices they've made.

"There is nothing more painful in human life than having to say goodbye to someone you love," he says, "but it becomes even more terrible if you have a disease like AIDS that some believe you got by being irresponsible. Too often, family and friends have already moved away from you and you die alone." Part of the work of the Caring Ministry is to try to reunite families torn apart by regrets. He says this healing is particularly necessary for former drug addicts.

"They don't spend time regretting the drugs they did," Giannone says. "They regret the times they were unkind to people, to their families, but they may feel it's too late to fix it." By surrounding them with love and dignity, Giannone says they are finally open to their own spiritual needs and are able to forgive and to accept forgiveness in return. "They find God's face," he says, and it's then that families can finally talk and heal. At that point, death becomes a release. "It's what you bring to the moment," he adds. "If you always cursed the darkness, your death could be dark. We fight that so that people don't take darkness to death, but instead bring light to it."

Atkinson has also seen hundreds of people die through his work in Third World countries, sometimes violently during civil war or through street violence, and sometimes through diseases that they contract through poverty and street living. He says it's interesting to note that in his experience, children who die have a very different journey than do many adults. He believes this is because they are closer to God.

"I've never been with a child who goes screaming and kicking," he says. "They seem to enter into this state of acceptance or transition. They definitely reach a point where they aren't afraid, and even if they're in pain, in the moments before death it seems to me that their pain is gone." He recalls children who died during Guatemala's civil war who were burned by phosphorous bombs and were moaning and obviously in severe pain who, at the very end, simply laid back and relaxed. He has seen the same thing at the Casa Jackson Home for Malnourished Infants in Antigua,

Guatemala. "It seems to me that their pain goes, they become peaceful and they enter into what can only be called a state of grace." Atkinson believes strongly in this time of transition. "It's not a light switch on-and-off type of moment," he adds. "More like moving from one phase to another."

For adults, the experience can be quite different. He has been in homeless shelters where people are dying of what he calls street living, typically of addictions that have destroyed their bodies, or they're poisoned from ingesting substances like turpentine. He says that most of the time they also seem to reach a state of resignation, as if they are turning themselves over to it. "It amazes me how many of them reach out for their mothers as they are dying," he says. He believes they've entered that transition phase and they see somebody waiting for them on the other side, as he did. Those deaths are peaceful. But it doesn't always happen that way.

"Some people are mean and nasty until the very end, bitter and angry," he says. For them, it's been his experience that their physical pain does not go away. They seem to carry it with them. They don't reach out, and if they mention God at all, it's not with love.

In the words of Pope Francis, when death happens this way, God weeps. "Jesus has wept for us! And that weeping of Jesus is exactly that of a father who weeps, who wants everybody with him." (Vatican Radio, 2-4-2014) Giannone says he and his fellow friars work hard to bring the dying into the light, drawing on the strength and mercy of God Himself, "to turn their tears into dancing."

Monsignor Patrick Schumacher is the pastor of a large parish. "People who have faith are more inclined to accept the grace to accept death," he says. "They accept that this world is temporary and we should enjoy it, but they know it's not the end and there is something more after this life. Still, the prospect of dying can be very frightening." He believes that the best way to prepare for death is in how you live. "You've prayed your prayers, you've been faithful, you've lived your life well, you've recognized your mistakes, confessed your failings, now put yourself in God's hands. That is why St. Benedict taught his monks, 'Keep death daily before your eyes.' (Rule 4.47)"

Frequently it is people like Giannone who, as Mother Theresa famously put it, "become a pencil in God's hands," who reach out to the dying and help to bestow God's grace.

Chapter 4

Glimpses of Life Beyond the Veil

Therefore, since we have been justified by faith, we have peace with God through our Lord Jesus Christ, through whom we have gained access to this grace in which we stand, and we boast in hope of the glory of God. –Romans 5, 1-2

My uncle was a heavy smoker who contracted lung cancer. Once his illness came to light, it quickly took over. As he died, he was essentially drowning in his own fluids - an admittedly scary experience - so his care team made sure that he had the medications he needed to be as comfortable as possible. One could argue that he was not aware of his surroundings as he drew his final breaths. But something beautiful happened.

"My dad was not responsive. He was heavily sedated and struggling to breathe," his son told me. "Suddenly, he sat up, reached out his arms and smiled, as if he was greeting somebody he loved." And then he died.

Wendy Rambaugh spent 18 years as a nurse, the last eight with hospice. She has been at the bedsides of hundreds of people, serving as a resource for families up to and beyond a patient's death, and what she has seen at those bedsides has cemented her belief in life after death.

"Almost everyone who can articulate at the end of their life sees someone who's coming for them or greeting them," she says. Often in the days before a person's death, she says they will have conversations with loved ones who have gone before, though she says people can be reluctant to talk about it for fear they won't be believed. But she believes. These experiences have convinced her that Heaven is closer than we think. The hours before death seem to open up our subconscious to things we normally can't see.

"They'll say, 'I spoke to Dad last night,' or someone else they care about," she says. "Hundreds of people have told me this, and though they worry that people will think they've lost their minds, they take great comfort from it." What's particularly interesting, she says, is that people who don't believe in God say the same thing. They often will see or talk to someone who has already passed away. "Most people do have a changed belief once they see someone from beyond," Rambaugh says. "They get a look in their eyes. They're looking at you, but it's like they're looking through you, too. They very commonly reach out. I was at the bedside of a man who knew he was dying and he was struggling with it. It was taking a long time. Finally he said, 'My brothers are here. They keep reaching for me.' I told him, 'The next time that happens, take their hands.' And the man died."

Lundblad often hears patients talking to someone whom the rest of the people in the room cannot see. And because patients feel safe with her, they will often tell her details about who they are seeing or hearing.

"One of our patients was sitting, talking to Jesus and to his own mom, who was deceased," she tells me. "He found great comfort in the conversations they were having, and it helped to prepare him. He was struggling to let go because he was trying to care for his wife. Those conversations helped bring him to a place of peace, with the understanding that the family would take care of his wife, so he could let go and be with Jesus and with his mother. The family got peace from those interactions, too, even though they couldn't see or hear them."

Lundblad relates another story of an elderly woman who was hospitalized, but not in serious condition, who called her aside to ask if she believed in angels. "I said, 'Yes, I do', and she said, 'Oh, good, because I've been seeing my grandma with someone.' We talked about it and I went out and checked her chart. She wasn't someone we thought was dying, so I wondered, 'What's going on here?' The next time I talked to her, her grandma was still there and I knew something was changing for her. The very next day she coded and she passed away a few days after that. There were no medical signs, but spiritually she had started her transition." Lundblad says it's been her experience that in the moments leading up to death, there can be a transition period where the veil between this world and the next becomes thin. "As in Acts when Stephen talks about seeing Jesus and the glory of Heaven," she says. "I think it's not just wishful thinking. We have some biblical basis to believe that it's possible."

Shea also believes that Heaven is closer than we think. "Some of the great saints have said that the battle between good and evil goes on around us all the time," he says. "We'd be amazed if we could just see it."

Lundblad agrees: "I think when you die it's a transition, which is why we see so many near-death experiences."

What about scientists who tell us that these experiences are merely metabolic changes in a brain that's shutting down? Lundblad doesn't necessarily disagree, but she takes it a step further. "The brain is part of our physical body, so the scientists are accurate, the brain *is* shutting down," she says. "But that doesn't mean our spirit doesn't continue to exist without the body." It doesn't mean that those experiences aren't real.

Doctors also sometimes try to explain people's deathbed behaviors by saying they're drug induced. Rambaugh doesn't think so. For one thing, she says the experiences that people have are individual to them. She tells a story of being at the bedside of a man who seemed to be struggling. He was thrashing about, churning his arms and legs, wiping his forehead and thrashing some more. It was very upsetting to his family members, who wanted her to give him something to settle him down. The man was a line worker with an electrical company, and she finally realized that he was climbing poles. She told him, "Grandpa, time for your coffee break," and the man lay still for exactly 15 minutes before starting up again. "It was comforting to the family to know he wasn't thrashing because he was in pain; he was actually working." She doesn't know why he was doing it, but she believes that for him it was part of the "work" of dying. She believes that this work is important and should not necessarily be medicated away. Because of this belief, she doesn't tend to give patients so much medication that they can no longer hear what's going on around them. In fact, she says hearing is the last sense to go. "Those are important moments," she says, and she doesn't believe that the patient or families should be deprived of them unless wakefulness is causing distress. And she further explains her belief that the so-called "visions" that people have are not drug induced. "We don't introduce those drugs just in the last weeks of life. Part of palliative care is giving people enough medication to keep them comfortable, but just enough. So those drugs have already been coursing through their systems. They don't see these things until the end, so I think it would be pretty rare that I'd attribute what people are seeing to meds."

"It really is interesting about professions," says Lundblad, who has had experiences similar to those that Rambaugh has seen. "We'll see electricians who are super busy with their hands, or they're looking for a piece that they need to put something together. What appears to be agitation might just be the patient working. Their mind continues to be busy." She says she'll ask families what has brought the patient comfort in the past, and when she tries that, they often settle down. "My own grandfather read the Bible through from beginning to end every single year, so when he was dying the only time he would be calm was when someone was reading scripture to him. We passed it around until everyone lost their voice, and that's how he spent his last weekend," she says. There's also the question: Why do some people have these experiences while others don't? "I think God gives us what we need to transition," she says. "Maybe that seems unfair to some, but not everyone needs that kind of experience in order to let go."

We must do the deeds of the one who sent me while it is day. The night comes on when no one can work -John 9:4

Some people have a strong caregiver instinct that makes it difficult to give in to dying. They don't want to cause pain to those around them, those whom they love. So they hang on longer than they might otherwise. Family members may become determined that their loved one will not die alone, so they set up a round-the-clock vigil. "One man I worked with was the head of a loving and devoted family," Rambaugh says, "and his daughter was so determined not to leave that she slept on his floor for an entire week. One night she couldn't be there, and that's the night he died."

"I think we can hold on to people and make them stay longer than they otherwise would," Lundblad says. "People may wait for that kid or that grandchild to get home when we think that medically it's impossible for them to hang on. That person comes or calls on the phone and then they let go."

Part of Lundblad's work at hospice is to help people who are struggling. "I'll ask them if there is somebody else they need to talk to, something they need to resolve. Are they waiting for something to happen?" She says talking this through is often enough to bring peace.

The first time my father-in-law started to die, my husband Cliff was alone with him in a hospital room. Gordon had been ill for years. Diabetic for most of his adult life, he had suffered a series of strokes that robbed him first of his mobility and eventually of his sight. He had become totally dependent on others, which was particularly difficult for a man who had been the breadwinner for a large family. On this day, he was suffering congestive heart failure and was not responding to the medicine that his doctors hoped would take some of the water weight off of his lungs.

As Gordon struggled for breath, his wife and the rest of his six children, their husbands, wives and kids were all at a lake in Minnesota, wrapping up a week at a resort. This was an annual tradition that Gordon himself had started, and it continues to this day. On this year there had been talk of canceling because, for the first time ever, Gordon wasn't well enough to attend and was in the hospital. But the family thought his wife, Harriet, needed a break, and there was no reason to believe that Gordon's health would reach a crisis on that particular weekend. Cliff remained with his father during that week while the rest of the family was away and was there when Gordon took a sudden turn for the worse. He called me from the hospital and with tears in his voice said, "Dad's taken a real downturn and the doctor was just here. He thinks he may not live for more than a couple of hours. You should tell everybody and get Mom back here."

Harriet didn't come alone. When they heard the news, the entire family went into high gear. They cleared the cabins and packed their vacation paraphernalia into vans, a task that normally takes all day, in just an hour and hit the road for the hour-and-a-half drive back to Fargo.

While he waited for his mother to arrive, Cliff sat with his dad, holding his hand. If Gordon was aware that Cliff was there, he didn't indicate it. He was essentially drowning, unable to clear fluid from his lungs or draw a deep breath. All of his energy went into inhaling and exhaling. Cliff wasn't sure how alert he was or whether he was frightened, so he did what he could to comfort him.

"I basically told him it was okay to go, that I understood how sick he'd been, how tough life had become for him," he told me. His vital signs continued to deteriorate. Cliff felt that his dad was tired of the effort involved in living in such a diminished capacity and was in need of rest. He believes that he was starting to die until he heard the sound of his wife's voice.

Harriet and all the children and grandchildren burst into the hospital, filling not only his room but every chair in the hall and waiting area, bringing their noise and energy with them. Each took a turn kissing Grandpa and telling him they loved him. Through all of the noise and confusion that can accompany a large family in crisis, I believe that Gordon heard one voice. Harriet was beside him and she begged him not to go.

Gordon was a railroad man. When I met him he was wearing striped overalls, and in all the years I knew him, I rarely saw him dressed in anything else. When I was pregnant with our first child, he gave me a pair because he said they were roomy and comfortable, and I wore them, too. Gordon was a good provider. But one thing that came hard to him was an outward show of affection. Like many men of his generation, he showed his care and concern through hard work. And on the day he was dying, he showed his love and devotion in the only way he could. He fought back death. Suddenly, with no good explanation, his lungs began to clear, and he went from grave, to critical, to stable within hours. He recovered to the degree where he was able to return home.

"I don't think it's always an easy step from this life to that," says Lundblad. "We hang on to this life so tightly, and families sometimes hang on even tighter than the patients."

Gordon lived for four more years. I can't say that they were particularly happy years, nor were they uncomplicated. There was no miracle cure of his disease. Instead, his condition continued to deteriorate to the point where he was forced to live in a nursing home, a place he truly hated. But it's also not for me to say that those years were a waste. These are things only God knows. What I can say is that when he finally died, Harriet was ready and loved him enough to let him go.

Lundblad tells of a hospital patient who was comatose after suffering a stroke. She was with staff as they talked to the man's wife about removing life support. "We knew it was their fiftieth wedding anniversary the next day," she says, "so we told her if she wanted to wait, they would understand. And she surprised us. She said, 'No, go ahead and do it now. He'll wake up and talk with me and he's going to dance with me again.' We tried to comfort her because we thought she was in denial, but in the end we did what she asked, thinking she would be disappointed. But she was completely right. After the tubes were removed he began to wake up and the last I saw him he was sitting up and talking. He left the hospital two weeks later."

Rambaugh and Lundblad both believe that people have a right to make decisions about their own lives, including the way they die, where they die and how much treatment they receive.

"I want people to know they have choices," Rambaugh says. "I want them to know they don't have to do things they aren't comfortable doing. Doctors find this dismaying. They are geared to save people no matter what, even if the treatments are futile." She says this causes families to run through savings and watch their loved ones suffer when there is really almost no chance for recovery. "The money that is spent in those last weeks of life is frightening to me. It takes people away from their families and puts a hardship on everybody." She believes that if all of us were more comfortable with the idea of death and what happens to us immediately afterward, these choices would be easier. But she agrees that it can be extremely difficult for people to sever those ties they've depended on.

"Spouses are often very tuned into each other, and they can surprise you," Lundblad says. "I've been with couples who go within a day of each other, even though one isn't sick. You really can die of a broken heart."

Ruth Opitz was known for her organizational skills. A devoted wife and mother, she survived breast cancer, not once, but twice. She was diagnosed the first time as a young mother and reacted to the news by fighting it with everything she had, but just in case, she also took the time to teach her 10-year-old daughter, Crystal, how to take care of herself and the family in the event that she didn't make it. She taught her how to cook and clean and run a household in an organized way. And then she didn't die. She lived to be 77 years old, and in the end it was a hospital-borne infection that killed her rather than the cancer. Though this time she was ready to let go, her husband Thomas was not. From the moment she passed away, he spent the rest of his life just waiting to join her. He would tell family, "The only reason God is waiting to take me is because He's waiting for Ruthie to get everything organized."

Ruth had a strong faith and did not fear death. The only reservation she had was one that Thomas shared. She didn't want to leave Thomas behind. She was in the ICU, and knew she was losing her fight, so she gathered her family around her as much as she could. Even in death, she was organizing events. Her son-in-law laughs when he tells me that she gave her son a list of songs that she liked. He was a talented guitar player and had a beautiful voice. He learned all the songs on the list and she told him that when the time came, she'd let him know which one to play. She finally narrowed it down to one, and not long afterward, as the family stood around her bedside, Ruth looked up and said, "Craig, it's time to play." When he got three-quarters of the way through the song she had chosen, she stopped breathing. Thomas died four years later, ready to join her. The experiences of those who have gone before tell us that she very likely was waiting to take his hand.

Chapter 5

Living Life Surrounded

"The great mistake of many people ... is to imagine that those whom death has taken, leave us. They do not leave us. They remain! Where are they? In the darkness? Oh, no. It is we who are in darkness. We do not see them, but they see us. Their eyes radiant with glory, are fixed upon our eyes ... Though invisible to us, our dead are not absent ... They are living near us transfigured into light and power and love." – Karl Rahner, S.J., Catholic Theologian

What a comforting thought! To know that someone we adore, though dead, remains with us as we continue our path through life. The Catholic faith has a tradition of asking the dead for help that goes back to the very beginning. We pray to the saints, asking for their intercession, and what are saints, really, but people who have found their way to Heaven? The Catholic Church teaches us that they are watching over us, and while involvement in our daily lives may not be obvious, they can reach out a helping hand when needed. It stands to reason, then, that our love does not die when we do, and those we love do not cease to care about us just because they've passed from this world to the next. Some of the people I interviewed for this book are absolutely convinced that they've been visited by a loved one who has passed away, sometimes within moments of their death and sometimes later. Sometimes the message they're trying to send is crystal clear, and sometimes not, but they don't doubt that what they've experienced is real.

"My brother was a mechanic in the Korean War," Harriet Naylor tells me. "I was quite a bit younger than he was, and even though he used to tease me and do the naughty things that older brothers do, I loved him very much, and he loved me. I missed him terribly when he was away at war and it was hard to be without him. I worried about him constantly and prayed for him all the time. One day I was cooking supper and I was clear across the room when a heavy cast-iron skillet flew off the stove and onto the floor. I had no explanation for it. It wasn't until days later that I found out my brother had died at exactly that moment."

Harriet is convinced that what happened in the kitchen was not a coincidence. She believes that her brother was trying to connect with her in some way shortly after his death, and though she wasn't aware at the time what was happening, she did take comfort later from the fact that he tried. Perhaps it was simply a sign that he was thinking of her, worrying about her as he died.

My mother tells of a night in her childhood when she awakened to the sound of her grandmother calling her name. "She lived in the house right across the alley behind us and I spent quite a bit of time with her. She was a music teacher, and she very patiently tried to teach me to play the piano. She was a constant in my life," she says.

When my mother was 17, her grandmother fell ill and was hospitalized. She remembers waking from a sound sleep because she distinctly heard her grandmother calling her name. It was disturbing enough that she couldn't go back to sleep, and a short time later the phone rang. It was the hospital calling, letting them know that her grandmother had passed away.

"It troubled me at the time," she says, "because I thought she needed me and I couldn't do anything to help her. I worried that she was afraid." But now she says it's possible that it was simply her grandmother thinking of her as she died.

Laura Holman also awakened to the sound of a loved one calling her, but this incident had a very real purpose. Her husband Bill had been deceased for about a year when she went on a trip with family members. She was sleeping one night at a bed and breakfast when she heard Bill, very close by, say, "Laura, get up!" She thought it was a dream, so she went back to sleep. But she heard it again, this time in a voice that she could not ignore: "Laura, get up NOW!" So she rose and got out of bed. She was groggy and disoriented, but gradually she became aware of a headache and nausea. She awakened the rest of the people in the house, because she somehow knew that she was suffering from carbon monoxide poisoning, and she was right. She believes that Bill saved not only her, but the rest of the family that night.

See, I am sending an angel before you, to guard you on the way—Exodus 23:20

Laura also talked of another time years earlier when Bill was still alive and she was visited by somebody trying to comfort her, although she had no idea who it was. She had gone in to see her doctor for a routine mammogram and they found a lump in her breast that her doctor was fairly certain was cancerous. She remembered being very frightened as she waited for her biopsy, sure that the news would be bad. Her doctor apologized to her when the tests came back, because the lump was not cancer after all, but a non-cancerous cyst.

When a second lump was discovered a couple of years later, she wasn't frightened at all, because she assumed that it was another cyst. On the night before her surgery, she was sound asleep beside Bill when she woke to the sound of someone's voice. She looked up and saw a man standing at the foot of her bed. She wasn't afraid of him, and somehow knew that he wasn't an intruder. She thought perhaps he was an angel, although she couldn't be sure. He told her in a comforting voice that this time she did have cancer, but that she need not fear because she would be just fine. Bill never woke up and said he had heard nothing when she asked him about it the next morning, so she was tempted to dismiss it as a dream, although it had felt very real. After her biopsy, her doctor again came into her room, but this time he told her that she did have breast cancer and he outlined a treatment plan that included surgery and radiation.

During the entire process, though she experienced the discomfort that came with the treatments, she was never scared and remained untroubled. And the apparition, if that's what it was, was right. She was completely cured of the disease. The remarkable thing, she later told me, was that feeling of calm, even after she received her diagnosis. She believed that whoever the man was who stood at the foot of her bed that night, he had been sent to reassure her, and her faith in the positive outcome was total.

Some people receive the gift of healing and some don't, just as bad things happen to good people, and why that is remains a mystery. Even though many of us say we want to die in our sleep or die instantly, sudden death does have the potential to rob us of important moments, and it can be just as hard on our loved ones as protracted illness. Some would say it's even harder, particularly if the death is a violent or painful one. We can't stand the thought that the person we loved suffered or was scared at the end.

Cathe Pittenger was plagued by this thought. Her daughter Sarah was murdered by her boyfriend when she was just 20 years old. Cathe's grief was profound and closure seemed impossible. About six months after Sarah died, Cathe says somebody rang her front doorbell. She went to answer it, but there was nobody there. When she walked away, it rang again. Still nobody. At that moment, the back doorbell rang twice. There was nobody there either, but Cathe says what was really strange was that her husband had disconnected the back doorbell when they changed the siding on the house and he'd never reconnected it. It was not working. Cathe is convinced that it was her daughter telling her that she was "still out there somewhere," and that she was okay.

Shea believes he has been aided by his little brother from beyond the grave. "Matthew and I were particularly close," he says. "When he was born I was at that pimply, awkward stage, and he gave me nonjudgmental affection. I used to lie on the floor and throw him into the air and he would laugh and laugh." Matthew, at four years old, was the youngest of seven boys born to Pat and Joe Shea. Too young for school, he missed all his brothers during the day when they were off at school, but he particularly missed Jim, who was the oldest. "When I went off to college that year, my mom told me that he would stand at the window and wait for me and say my name."

The year was 1994, and Shea was a freshman at Jamestown College, a school a couple of hours away from the family farm in Hazelton, North Dakota. Matthew had been missing his brothers all day, waiting for the school day to end so that he could go outside and play. The Shea farm was at the top of a hill. When the boys came home, they dressed Matthew in his snowsuit and took him outside to do some sledding. Their dad was on the tractor, moving snow at the bottom of the hill, and he told the boys to wait. But Matthew, either too excited or because he hadn't heard, suddenly threw himself onto the sled and started down the hill before his brothers could catch him. When he reached the bottom of the hill, he slid under the back wheel of the moving tractor. It all happened in a moment.

"One of the boys ran into the house to call Mom, and Steve called 911, but the ambulance was in Linton and it took about 15 minutes to come. Dad and Mom picked Matthew up and started driving to meet the ambulance. Mom held him while Dad drove, saying the whole time that he hadn't meant to do it. And they prayed the Rosary. They met the ambulance about halfway, but there was really nothing they could do. His skull was crushed."

He remembers that his mother was the one who called him at school and said, simply, "Matthew's gone." She told him there'd been an accident and that he needed to come home. He says he didn't react at first. "What I did was go into the bathroom and shave," he says. "I suppose I was numb and in shock." Then the pastoral minister at the school drove him home to the farm.

At first the family's grief was overwhelming, but with time they felt comforted, and their strong faith helped. They also believe that Matthew did what he could to comfort them. Twice, Pat dreamed that he was with her and that she was holding him. She believes he truly was with her in those moments. The boys who had been with Matthew when he died struggled with their grief, each in his own way, not really getting over it, but learning to live with it. Two years later, something amazing happened.

In the same month that Matthew died, Pat became pregnant again. She was 44 at the time, and had thought she was in menopause. Nine months later, she gave birth to Maria, a long-awaited little girl. Shea believes that Maria was a special gift, influenced by Matthew, and he says the little boy's death brought the entire family closer together. Their faith is what got them through, and it became stronger with time. He says the experience is probably what set him on the path to the priesthood. But it didn't end there.

"I was a young country priest, happy in my role and quite content," he says, when he received word that he was under consideration to be the president of the University of Mary, a position that would make him the youngest university president in the country. "I knew that if I took this job I would have a great life in terms of doing great things, but I also realized I'd never have that quiet life again, a life I loved. It was a time of upheaval for me and considerable confusion."

He was teaching at Dickinson Trinity High School at the time. "There was this one kid," he says. "At the beginning of the term I would grab the yearbook and memorize the students' names and faces. I always amazed them because on the first day I knew who they were. But I couldn't remember this one kid. His dad would come in for parent-teacher conferences and I'd just say, 'Your son is doing fine,' because I couldn't remember him. Who is this kid? But one day a paper he wrote caught my attention and it reminded me of Matthew, and suddenly I realized that this boy reminded me of my little brother and even looked like him. I think that was Matthew making me aware that he was praying for me, by making me aware of this boy. I know he's there for me. It's not a matter of belief for me, it's a matter of knowledge. I believe he was offering me consolation at a time of upheaval."

Out of the depths I cry to You, O Lord—Psalm 130:1

A man I knew lost his son Patrick in a tragic, yet foolish accident. "When I get to the great beyond and I see Patrick," he once said to me, "I don't know if I'll first hug him or smack him for being so stupid."

Patrick was in college and living at a fraternity house that backed onto a railroad siding. It was a track that was rarely used, and as a hobby the boys would keep a record of the train schedule. They thought they knew which nights the trains would come through. One night the frat house hosted a party, and Patrick had classes the next day. It was noisy in the house and he was looking for a quiet place to sleep. It had rained earlier, so the ground was soggy. Looking around, he saw that the tracks were dry, so he unrolled his sleeping bag between the rails and went to sleep. In the wee hours of the morning, a train came through unexpectedly and killed him.

"That night, before I knew that my son was dead my wife (who had died several years earlier) visited not just me, but my older sons, too, each of us in a dream," my friend says. "The dreams were different, but they all followed the same idea." He said he dreamed that he was in the laundry room of his house and his wife was suddenly there and she said to him, "Don't worry about Patrick, he's with me." It wasn't until later, when he mentioned the dream to his sons, that they all said they'd had similar dreams on the same night. He believed that his wife, out of love for them all, came to them to comfort them.

My friend Beverly is convinced that her husband, Peter, visited her often in the days and weeks following his sudden death from suicide. At the time she felt inconsolable, but her grief warred with her anger and disbelief. She was trying to deal with her incredible hurt while also trying to comfort and raise her devastated young daughters. She felt his presence constantly, felt his regret, but took no comfort from it. She thought, instead, that he was meddling in her life and the lives of her children, and that he no longer had that right. She lost a great deal of weight, as often happens when people are grieving. She kept a scale in her bathroom, and whenever she weighed herself she noticed that the weight on the scale was set with several pounds already registered. At first she didn't pay much attention, and would simply put the scale back to zero and move on with her day. But every morning it would be forward a few pounds past the zero mark when she went to step on it. She thought at first that the children were playing with it, so she hid it in the closet, but the result was always the same, always a few pounds off of zero. It finally occurred to her that Peter was worried about her and was trying to tell her to stop losing weight.

"And he was right, I was not taking care of myself," she says. "For a while I really did contemplate whether life was worth living." She believes that she was visited by the Angel of Death, and though she didn't have a classic near-death experience and didn't contemplate ending her own life, she believes that she did have a choice of whether to go on or to simply to give up and die.

"If it wasn't for my girls, I don't know what my decision would have been," she says. But she does believe that her husband's presence remained with her for many months until she met the man she would eventually marry.

"I was in bed not really asleep, just dozing, and I felt somebody sit down on the bed next to me," she says. "There was a definite dip. I thought it was the cat. But when I opened my eyes, nobody was there. At that moment I felt an enormous sense of peace, and I believe it was his way of telling me that he thought I was in good hands. I never felt his presence again." What she feels instead, she says, is the loving presence of God in her life.

Chapter 6

When Fear Fades

Heaven, the Father's house, is the true homeland toward which we are heading and to which, already we belong. – Catechism of the Catholic Church, 2802

Few things fascinate quite like the near-death experience. It offers comfort and for those who experience it, it can serve to sweep away some of those clouds of mystery that surround death and dying. The sense of comfort that a near-death experience offers likely explains the popularity of books that describe them, and the journeys that people take can be quite detailed and can feel very lengthy. But nearly dying isn't the same as dying, because you come back. For that reason, we can't be absolutely sure that the experience wasn't some trick of the dying brain, as many scientists insist. Despite Patrick Atkinson's assurance that those who have the experience know it for what it is and have no doubt that it's real, the rest of us have to take it on faith. A friend told me that he sat with his father-in-law, Joe, as he lay dying. Joe was not a man of faith and he wasn't looking for God. His final words were: "You know what they say about seeing the light? Well, it's BS." And then his heart stopped. But then, his wasn't a near-death experience because he *did* die, so what happened after he left his body is a matter for speculation. Perhaps he went on to travel the tunnel toward the light that so many describe. Or perhaps he simply closed his eyes in this world and opened them in the next.

But those who do have the experience seem to have one thing in common. Like Atkinson, they lose their fear of death, and it's very difficult to convince them that what they felt was a trick of oxygen-starved cells or of synapses when they stop firing. In fact, in some ways, they begin to look forward to that day. It can be a true gift.

My Aunt Isabel spoke of this. Hers was a very busy life. She not only was the mother to five girls, but her husband was also ill with multiple sclerosis. There were a lot of people depending on her. She woke up one morning with a headache that seemed to grow worse as the day went on, but she and her husband, Tom, had plans that night to have dinner in a restaurant with Louis, a family friend. They kept those plans. But as the evening wore on, she felt steadily worse and finally said she needed to go out for air. Shortly afterward, she collapsed. Tom was wheelchair bound, and while he could drive a car that was specially outfitted for him, they hadn't driven that car to the restaurant that night. Louis told Tom that he would take Isabel to the hospital. Meanwhile, Tom called his oldest daughter, Maria, then 16 years old, to come and pick him up.

Louis took Isabel to the closest hospital, but the emergency physicians realized right away that she needed a neurosurgeon, that she had bleeding in her brain from what would later be determined was a burst aneurysm, and they arranged a transfer to another hospital. While she was being evaluated, she was not conscious, but later, she was able to describe not only what was going on in her room and the care she was receiving, but what was happening in the next room as well. She had the classic experience of drifting outside her body and looking down on the doctors as they worked on her.

Shortly after arriving at the first hospital, she was taken by ambulance to another better-equipped facility where she was prepped for surgery. Tom and Maria went first to one hospital, and then to the second, and afterward, Tom refused to leave her side, and later described how her heartbeat would spike at the sound of his voice, and again when the doctor talked about cutting off her long black hair and shaving her head.

At some point during that night, perhaps during surgery, perhaps before, Isabel had what has become known as a classic near-death experience. She saw the white light and the tunnel and had the sense of traveling. She felt the peace of her surroundings and was given a choice. She could stay, or she could go. She said afterward that she wanted very much to go toward that light, but in the end she fought her way back because there were so many people depending on her –her husband and her five young children.

She was told not long after the first surgery that she had another aneurysm, and that she should probably have yet another surgery to eliminate it, as it could also rupture at any time. She chose not to have that surgery, saying that death didn't frighten her, but that the potential complications from the surgery did. She told the doctor she would take her chances. Isabel died years later from pancreatic cancer. Her daughter told me it's not accurate to say that Isabel looked forward to death, because she didn't want to leave her children and grandchildren behind, but from what Isabel told me, I don't believe that death itself frightened her.

Her experience of seeing what was going on around her while she was unconscious is far from unique. Schumacher mentions studies where numbers or colors are put on top of cabinets in trauma rooms and people can tell their trauma team exactly what's on top of the cabinets; they see things that they couldn't possibly know.

Scott McFall had this experience during surgery when he was 11 years old. Like Isabel, he could describe the surgery itself and what others in the room were doing and saying. He says there was nothing about it that seemed dreamlike. He says there was never any doubt in his mind that the experience was real.

"You'll find a lot of medical personnel who've had those types of conversations, for instance, with kids who can talk about their surgeries. There are people who try to explain it away. They'll say you're waking up and hearing things and that you've constructed the visuals to go with it, but when you have it happen to you, you're certain you didn't make it up."

"What's happening is a separation of the body and the soul," says Schumacher. "The soul is leaving the body. Families who have been at the bedside have reported to me that they've seen a blue light at the moment of a loved one's death. People can probably deny that there's light at the end of the tunnel, that it's just the brain shutting down, but you can't deny that people have had near-death experiences." Plus, it's one thing to think that the dying person is hallucinating, but it's harder to dismiss it when loved ones around the bed all experience the same thing, such as that blue light or a light mist or a presence -- all things reported over and over again by people standing vigil at the bedsides of the dying. "There are too many people who've had the experiences to just dismiss them all," Schumacher says.

Do not let your hearts be troubled—John 14:1

We can and do take comfort from hearing about experiences like Isabel's, but because we aren't all blessed with that kind of assurance, the fear of the unknown remains, and it can impact people on a lot of levels. The job of a pastor, a teacher, a spiritual adviser or a counselor can be to help talk us through some of those fears.

First may be our fear of the physical pain that often accompanies death. That's why you hear so often that people want to die in their sleep. They believe that they want to go quickly, and really, few of us want to linger if we know that we'll feel sick and miserable. Father Paul Becker is a parish priest who visits often with the dying. He says humans approach death on multiple dimensions, be they physical, emotional, social, mental or spiritual, but that each individual tends to dwell on a particular aspect. He has found that getting to the bottom of the fear and then helping a person deal with that specific thing can often bring great comfort to the dying. For example, if a person's fear is physical, he points out that medications can do a great deal to lessen or even eliminate pain.

When the fear is emotional, he says it's important to find the source of the mental turmoil. The dying person may feel a sense of impending loss. There is that fear of leaving people un-provided for. But he believes that an even greater fear might be, "How will *I* do without *them*? Will I be forgotten?" When Becker talks with people who have this worry, he reminds them that love is the one sense that transcends death. Your love goes with you when you die. "Scripture tells us that within a blink of an eye, we'll be reunited with those we love," he says. "We'll be connected with everybody we love; they'll be there with us, although the nature of those connections may change. Or, to put it another way, here on earth there may be three people who truly love you. How good does that feel? Now imagine there are legions of people who truly love you. How good is that? Our love on earth is narrow and actually reflects our dependency. It will be different in the next life, where we'll have the freedom to love completely."

Becker says many people tell him that they're afraid of losing all of the things they love to do when they die. He says the thing he does in those cases is help people focus on the reality of the here and now. "Say you love to go camping," he says. "When you're ill and approaching death, is that physically possible for you? You've likely lost those things already, so don't let the memory of them hold you here."

People also worry that they might be bored in Heaven; the idea that we'll all be sitting around on clouds worshipping God for all eternity does sound pretty boring. Most people would rather be busy, especially in this day and age when we're frantically moving from one activity to the next. But does your busyness make you happy, or does it just keep you occupied? If somebody tells us that we won't have the need for busyness because we'll be content, we really can't fathom it. What's needed, Becker says, is trust, and trust is hard. "I remind people that whatever they think they can describe about Heaven, about God, is probably wrong. We can't know because we can't take it all in. We're too limited. We just know it will be good. So the answer to the question of 'Will I be bored?' is no. 'What will I do?' Doesn't matter. It will be good. Relax and don't worry. Just trust. Don't try to take the experiences you know here and apply them to Heaven, because you can't." He counsels people to think of a time here on earth when they felt totally loved and cared about. In Heaven, you'll have that all the time.

Becker says some people try to think their way through the dying experience. They are more comfortable with thought processes than with feelings. They try to puzzle it out as if it's a scientific problem they can solve. Death becomes a mental construct. Of course, we can't truly get to the bottom of it until it happens, but he says allowing these people to discuss it sometimes helps.

And then there is the spiritual aspect of dying and preparing for death. Becker does talk with people who feel that they don't deserve Heaven, despite what we're taught: that God loves us no matter what and Jesus forgives our sins if we ask Him to. Perhaps they can't forgive themselves for the things they've done and they feel that God won't forgive them either.

"I'd ask that person to tell me what they think will get them to Heaven. Is it faith? How does God decide who has faith? Do they believe that God loves them? Do they believe that their mistakes are so big that God can't forgive them? Then I remind them that God is not a policeman. He's not sitting in wait, ready to pounce on people at the first sign of weakness. God wants to love us no matter what. We just have to accept that love.

"You hold on to the things you know because the unknown is so frightening, even if you think it will be good," he says. "We tend to project our understandings and our human qualities onto God because we can't really understand Him. That's what the Old Testament was really all about. God invites. You make the choice of what to do with that invitation."

according to thy word; the Presentation – dismiss your servant Lord; the Agony in the Garden – if it's Thy will, let this cup pass from me, but not my will but Yours be done; the Crucifixion – Into Your hands I commend my spirit; and finally, the Resurrection. I've seen that bring more peace than most things do. A sense of calm descends and people seem to accept God's will," he told me.

When a person nearing death would tell him that they were afraid to let go because they didn't want to cease to "be," he would offer words of comfort and assurance, telling them that feeling that way was itself proof of God's love. You will always be "you" because God created you, and "God thinks you're important." He knew that his own life was coming to an end, and he clearly found the waiting difficult, but he also had faith that he would live on as Tom Kramer, the person whom God created.

Chapter 7

Where is God When Death is Hard?

I am indeed going to prepare a place for you, and then I shall come back to take you with me, that where I am you also may be. —John 14:3

Deb Carpenter's childhood was so normal, so traditional as to be almost cliché, except it was better than most because her parents were better than most. She was the fourth daughter born to Edwin and Magdaline Steinert, an unplanned but much loved last child growing up in the 60s and 70s in a small town in middle America. Ed was born in 1919 on a farm near Regan, North Dakota. That's where he learned his values of hard work and steadfast loyalty, and it's where he began his married life with Maggie. He was 22 and she was 20 when they wed. Both came from large families. He was the youngest of 11, Maggie was the youngest of 12, and they were well suited to family life and to one another.

"My parents never fought," says Deb. "My dad was a gentle giant, very soft spoken. Say my mom made something for dinner that he didn't like. The worst thing he could say was, 'Well, I wouldn't want it every day.' And he and my mother always put the children first, which at the time was kind of unusual, I think." He loved all his girls, but when Deb came along late and by surprise, she says she was her father's last chance to have a tomboy, and she became his companion. By then the family lived in Bismarck, where Maggie was a homemaker and Ed began a 40-year career as a mechanic for a local car dealership. Her sisters were nearly grown by the time she was born, so in a way it was as if she was an only child, and Ed doted on her.

"He never had to raise his voice or punish me," she says. "If I did something wrong his eyes would well up with tears and he'd say, 'I'm so disappointed.' I would rather he had hit me, that's how bad I'd feel. But it worked."

Deb stayed close after she grew up, going away to the University of North Dakota to study law, but then settling back in her hometown, not far from her parents. For most of those years, Ed was the sweet-tempered father she'd always known. But as he neared the end of his life, a series of ailments began to plague him. He'd injured himself in a fall shortly after his retirement that remained bothersome. He had a brain bleed that required surgery, along with mini strokes. The changes in his brain changed his personality. Deb says he no longer had a filter and would say whatever was on his mind. "He would say things that weren't very kind," Deb says. "I am very much like him and so when he said those things I clashed with him."

He got shingles, not just once, but five times in four years. The pain from that tormented him. Finally, in the last year of his life he got an infection in his foot.

"He'd complained a lot about pain from the shingles and he had other aches and pains that he talked about, too. So much so, that we got used to it. At first, when he talked about how much his foot hurt, we didn't pay much attention," Deb says with regret. By the time they did focus on his foot, the leg itself was gangrenous and had to be amputated above the knee. After that he lost his mobility and was discharged to a nursing home, but he never really recovered. "I tortured myself with guilt over it," Deb says. "What if I'd looked at that leg a week earlier?"

Guilt is such a common reaction when a loved one dies. So often we ask ourselves what we could have done differently, but the answer is usually not much. Dick Heidt's father died at the age of 72, but he'd been ill for nearly a decade before that with Alzheimer's Disease. The family cared for him at home for six and a half years until he lost the ability to walk. At that point there was nothing left to do but take him to a nursing home. The family visited often for the final year and a half of his life, even though he didn't know them and didn't seem to get much from the visits. Dick says it was tough to watch him continue to deteriorate because he seemed to be in pain, yet he couldn't tell his family or caregivers what was wrong. When his dad finally died, Dick thought he would be ready. He'd had years to prepare for it.

"While I thought it would be best that he died in the latter days of his life, his death really threw me for a loop," he says. "I had more grief than I expected, even though I felt it was for the best. I'm guessing it was the relief from a long and trying time for my family."

Deb agrees. "You may feel it's for the best; there's an acceptance that death ends the suffering. But you have to choose faith and joy, because at the time you won't feel it. You have to trust. Faith isn't built when things are going well, it's built when they aren't."

I felt guilt when my father died, too. Getting to his home was time consuming and expensive, and I had a limited amount of vacation, which meant for years I saw him only once a year. During that last visit before his death, I remained with him only a few days, and then took some time afterward to vacation in a nearby city. Had I realized that would be my last visit, I still ask myself if I would have remained with him for those extra days. It wasn't long afterward that he went into rapid decline, going first to the hospital and then transitional care, where his personality changed from always sweet and loving toward me to angry and frustrated. The conversations about life and loved ones that I'd had with him on that final visit never happened again. I had to talk to him via cellphone where reception was spotty. He had a roommate and the television was always blaring. We had difficulty understanding each other and the calls often ended with him simply handing the phone off to somebody else. When I could hear, it was a litany of complaints, and I wasn't sure how much of it was true and how much of it was happening in his overly-anxious brain. What he was waiting for so desperately was for his doctor to visit and authorize his discharge. Without that, he said, his insurance would not pay the bill. Day after day he told me the doctor had still not come. When I offered to contact the administration he became angry with me, certain that they would retaliate by keeping him "locked up" for a longer time.

It's a difficult role we find ourselves in when we have to begin parenting our parents. We're so conditioned to lean on them. When the roles reverse, we often don't know how to handle it. I was not ready or able to defy my father's wishes, even though I thought a good conversation with the facility staff would be in his best interest. And Deb found it difficult, too. "I was not ready for that role reversal," she says.

During his final illness, Ed Steinert was angry. He developed a condition called hospital psychosis and was starting to see things that weren't there, which is very common, but it also was unnerving for the family.

"He was sometimes sweet, but most of the time he was just angry. So angry. He would be yelling at someone, and he kept trying to take his clothes off," almost as if he was trying to escape. And Deb believes that's exactly what he was trying to do. Like my father, he didn't want to be where he was any longer, but didn't know how to make his suffering end. "I never questioned that Dad was going to a better place. I don't think he questioned it, either," Deb tells me. "He was angry that he was being kept here. I think he saw us as obstacles to his leaving," she says. But she also realizes that had he not been sick, he would never have reacted that way. "He really was not my dad anymore," she adds.

Hospice workers have told me that death itself is usually not difficult or painful. But the days and hours leading up to it can be very tough, not just on the patient, but on the whole family. It can be hard in those times to recognize a caring, loving God, and it's often then that people question His very existence. They ask, "Why is God allowing this suffering?"

"But is God making it happen?" asks Donna Dohrmann, a retired ELCA minister. "Rather than inflicting things on us, I think he accompanies us on our journey," she says. "He gives us strength and hope in the midst of our hardship and surrounds us with his love. And when we die, I believe God weeps.

"It would be a deist god who watches us from a distance and doesn't get involved. If we follow God all the way through Adam and Eve and Abraham and David to Jesus, you can see that we do not have a deist god. He's always been very involved in the lives of men. He is never distant."

Then why does God heal some of us but not others, even when we pray for it so fervently? She says it depends on how you view "healing."

"The ultimate healing is going home to Jesus," says Dohrmann. "As for the rest, God gave us eternal life, but He gave us finite bodies."

Deb's dad died on a Saturday. Maggie had been visiting him as she did every day. Deb had been there earlier.

"I don't think she had made it out of the parking lot before the nursing home called me," Deb says. "They wanted to send Dad to the E.R. but I said no, he's had enough. He'd been in the hospital for hours just the day before where they'd tried to start an IV for fluids and it was a painful fiasco. I didn't want to put him through it again. When I told them that, they said we should come right away." By the time Deb and her mother got back to the nursing home, he had already died.

"I think he was more comfortable going when Mom and I were not there," says Deb. Again, it's a choice many people make in their final moments.

My grandmother was a perfect example of someone who had grown bored with living and simply waited for her life on this earth to be over. She could no longer hear, and couldn't see well enough to entertain herself with the things that once brought her pleasure, like knitting and reading. Her days seemed to stretch on forever. She had signed a "Do Not Resuscitate" order and was ready and waiting for the moment when death would decide to take her. But when she was brought to the hospital in her final illness, the paperwork wasn't immediately available. Her heart was slowing and she was actually crossing over to the other side when the hospital called her son to ask what they should do.

We tend to panic in those situations. My uncle, wanting what was best for her but unwilling or unable to make the final decision, told the trauma team to do everything they could to save her. The thing was, though, she didn't want saving for this life. Rather, she wanted to be rescued from it. As soon as she regained lucidity she looked my mother in the eye and said almost angrily, "Why didn't you let me go?" Mom hadn't been there for the decision and could only apologize. My grandmother died a short time later.

How blessed are the poor in spirit; the reign of God is theirs – Matthew, 5:3

Richter says it's also important to remember that our lives don't really belong to us. That, he says, is what it means to be poor in spirit. Famous American author and Catholic mystic, Thomas Merton, said that once you understand and accept this and really begin to believe it, your attitudes may change. He wrote in his book, *The Seven Storey Mountain*, "Everything belongs to God. We possess nothing, not even our lives. And when we realize this and give ourselves over to God for safekeeping, it takes some of the anxiety out of living, and out of dying."

Not only does God walk with you, the Bible tells us others do too:

Therefore, since we for our part are surrounded by this cloud of witnesses, let us lay aside every encumbrance of sin, which clings to us and persevere in running the race which lies ahead. - Hebrews 12:1

Chapter 8

The Sacrament of the Sick

"Pray, hope and don't worry. Worry is useless. God is merciful and will hear your prayer." – Padre Pio

My father spent most of his last month of life in a place he never wanted to be. He had grown weak because of an infection that wouldn't clear. His doctor thought his best chance was to go to an assisted living facility where he could receive physical therapy in the hope that it would build up his strength enough to go home. He agreed, but only because he couldn't walk. From the moment he entered, he had his eye on the exit sign. He did what was asked of him in terms of physical therapy, but I don't believe he became physically stronger. I believe it was sheer strength of will to go home that allowed him to walk down the hallway far enough to be considered "well."

When he was finally discharged, he spent his entire first night at home sitting up in his favorite chair, with his remote by his side, doing what he had for weeks been denied the chance to do. He watched a ball game and then the all-night news, on his own schedule. When I spoke with him that day on the phone, he sounded weak but content.

But he was not cured. A few mornings later, although he rose from bed and made it to the kitchen table, he was not able to rise again. His wife, Karen, asked him what he wanted her to do, and he told her to call the doctor. She said, "You know what he'll say." And my father, with resignation, said, "He'll tell me to go to the hospital." I truly believe that he would have stayed right where he was, except for one thing. He accepted that last ambulance ride because he didn't want his wife to have to watch him die while she was alone with him. In the emergency room he quickly deteriorated, and to help him breathe he was intubated and put on a respirator. From then on he was sedated and never regained consciousness. His final words were to the hospital staff when he said, "Do whatever you have to do."

My brother and I live far away in different states, and the community where my father lived was not easy to reach. It required hours of travel, so when Karen called to say we should come right away, it took us a day and a half to get there. In that time we called frequently, checking on him in the ICU, where he was fighting pneumonia along with congestive heart failure and an uncontrolled cardiac rhythm. My brother and I knew that my father had not been to Mass, or even to church in a long time, but we felt certain that he would want a priest to administer the last rites. A Catholic priest was not available, so my brother contacted an Episcopal priest, who was at the hospital within an hour.

My brother is Episcopalian and was satisfied with that, and I felt, too, that God would not stand on rules. But even so, I later felt the need to visit with a priest, who said not to worry. Father Josh Ehli told me, "God knows what's in your heart, your desire to be with Him. God, working through the Church, never gives up on people, and so many things can happen at the moment of death that are beyond our awareness. What is most important is that we seek God's abundant mercy every day, if possible, and most importantly, at the moment of death."

Ehli says there are no coincidences in death, and as luck would have it, in the weeks after my father's passing, he delivered a sermon that I was privileged to hear, on what is now called the Sacrament of the Anointing of the Sick. In it, he explained that the sacrament used to be called Extreme Unction, but has undergone a name change to encompass a broader purpose. You don't have to be dying, necessarily, to receive it; you simply need to be in danger. This can include a serious illness or surgery, serious mental illness or addiction. And you can have the sacrament more than once.

"There seems to be a notion that if I call the priest and he comes and anoints me, it will kill me," Ehli later told me with a smile. "People think, 'I don't want to call because I don't want to die right now.' I can assure you, the sacrament has never killed anyone."

He says you don't have to ask for the sacrament yourself, as in the case of my father. Those who surround the person can ask on his or her behalf. "If our loved ones think we kind of, a little bit, would like to go to Heaven? Call the priest."

But it goes even further than that. Suppose there is no Catholic priest available, again, as in the case of my father. Ehli says that the desire to have a priest present, the desire to receive God's mercy through the sacraments even when a priest cannot arrive in time, is known to God. "God always works in the sacraments. That's what they are here for, to give us the assurances of God's saving power, but God is always free to work outside the sacraments as well."

Because my father had not been practicing his faith and had not been going to Sunday Mass, Church law says he may have died in mortal sin. But the Church does not require you to be in a state of grace to receive the sacrament. "If you had eight million mortal sins on your soul, and your family or spouse knows you would want to be forgiven, that's all God needs," Ehli says. "Just a little desire from you for Heaven, and His mercy can destroy eight million sins."

If all that is true, and God knows what's in your heart, why bother with the sacrament at all? The simple answer is that it gives you strength for the journey. When you are at your weakest, and least able to defend yourself, when you are suffering and in pain, that's when you are most vulnerable.

"Who comes a-knocking?" Ehli asks. "The evil one, because he's a bully. God knows that, and that's why He gave us the sacrament. You get the strength to tell the evil one to hit the road."

Catholics do not believe that the sacrament is absolutely required for entry into Heaven, but Ehli says it does offer the dying a kind of certainty and peace in their final moments, especially when the Sacrament of Reconciliation cannot be received earlier. "God can overcome anything and He can read your heart, but why not relax into that peace as you face the final journey?" he says.

A priest can also bestow an Apostolic Pardon, and Catholic teaching says that no matter what you've done, the doors of Heaven can be opened for you. This can be a great comfort to the dying, particularly those who have lived with the fear of purgatory. Ehli explains it this way: "After forgiving your sins and strengthening you, the Church can open up the treasures of Heaven for you, call on the saints, the martyrs and the very power of Jesus Christ Himself, who says, 'I want you in Heaven.' He wants nothing more than to have you there with Him and, through the victory won by the sufferings of Christ, He can make it happen, even to the point of bypassing the necessary purifications of purgatory. His love and mercy are that powerful."

Be on guard, therefore. the Son of Man will come when you least expect Him - Luke 12:40

When it comes to death, the best defense against fear is to live each day as if it's your last because it could be. Cardinal Joseph Bernardin said in his book *Gift of Peace* that you should "pray while you're well because if you wait until you're sick you might not be able to do it." I have no idea if my father prayed at the end of his life, but I know I prayed for him, both before and after his death. The Episcopal priest prayed for him, and so did my brother. My faith in God tells me that it was enough.

Chapter 9

The Rituals Surrounding Death

Fear of death makes us devoid of valour and religion. For want of valour is want of religious faith. – Mahatma Gandhi

What is it about final wishes? Why do we feel that we have to obey them? Dad did not want a funeral. So uncomfortable was he with the whole idea of death and the grief it would cause for those he loved that he asked that there be no services whatsoever. The closest we came to ritual during the week after his passing was to visit the funeral home to arrange for his cremation and choose a container for his ashes. At some point in the past he had told his wife that he wanted his ashes scattered on the Missouri River where he had spent so many happy hours fishing. That probably seems a reasonable request except for the fact that it went against everything I believe to be sacred. Scattering ashes is likely well-meant and seems like a romantic and moving thing to do. I don't mean to judge those who choose to do it, but I've heard too many disturbing stories when things didn't go well. A friend told me she scattered her husband's ashes in a stream, only to have them blow back into her face. She could feel the grit in her teeth. I've known people who couldn't decide on the perfect place and instead left relatives' remains on their fireplace mantels for months into years. One acquaintance told me she parceled out her grandmother's ashes to people who attended the funeral as a kind of keepsake, so that all of them could keep Grandma close. And one particularly gruesome story had the deceased's finger bone leave the urn intact during a scattering ceremony. The minister who was presiding deliberately put his foot over it so that the guests wouldn't see it and be disturbed.

I believe there is a reason for the rituals surrounding death; even the earliest humans observed them. In my case, the lack of a funeral made the event seem less real somehow. We had a gathering in a motel room of close family members and friends. It was a little like an old-fashioned Irish wake, but for me it brought no closure. It made me think: What if one does not feel bound to honor a loved one's last wishes? It was a question that I put to Schumacher. "It's a funny thing," he told me. "When you're alive, if you have a bad idea, I can argue with you and tell you how you are in error. The minute a person dies, we seem to think their final wishes are more sacred than scripture, no matter how misguided. But here's the thing: If it's a bad idea, we don't have to honor it."

Schumacher has presided at nearly 650 funerals and is a firm believer in the importance of the rituals that surround death. He's a believer in the importance of an open casket as well. "People need to view the body," he says. "It's a last gift you can give your loved ones. It's not about you; you're dead. It's to help them with their grieving process, and it's an important part," just as the funeral and the blessings that happen at the graveside are important. He is not a fan of cremation, but he says, "Even if you're cremated, at least bury the cremains so there is a place of rest and a point of memory and respect for those who loved you and need to grieve."

When Matthew Shea died, his father dug his grave himself. It wasn't a fast process; it took hours, over more than one day, and while he had help, it was an important last service that he could perform for his son. It helped to ease his sorrow, and while nobody blamed him for the accident that took his little boy's life, it helped to ease his guilt. "I suppose that was his way of atoning," says Shea. "And I planned his funeral."

"We embalm bodies to give families time to come to terms with the death," says Schumacher. "We need time to accept what's happened. And we need to spend time with the body. The grieving process takes days to really begin. Every aspect of funeral planning has a purpose, from the initial visit that the pastor may make to a grieving family's home, to the planning of the service, to the visitation, the vigil, the funeral itself and the burial; even the funeral lunch that follows has an important purpose. It's all part of a last service of love that people can perform, and it helps them come to terms with a loved one's passing from their lives. Let me put it this way: Unresolved grief does weird things to people, often unconsciously and permanently."

Although the Catholic Church allows it, Schumacher believes that cremation slows the grieving process and may even permanently disrupt it. Richter points out that when the body is cremated, families put a picture of the deceased person beside the urn. "We want something to look at," he says. "I hear people say, 'I don't want people looking at me after I'm dead,' but really, that's about you. Remember, the presence of the body is for those grieving, not the deceased."

"The Catholic funeral rite is a beautiful ritual, and the ritual is comforting in itself," Father John Guthrie says. "Connectivity is crucial when somebody dies. As individualistic as our culture is, people crave connection. This is why death is so fearful. It's a radical alienation on an existential level."

Guthrie sees cremation as a violent act, one that deprives the family and the community of an essential part of the mourning process. Still, more and more people are choosing cremation for a variety of reasons, not the least of which is expense. But there are rules that surround it. The Church would not advise a Catholic to scatter ashes on the Missouri River because the Church teaches that the body is sacred.

My brother and I spent a lot of time discussing what to do to honor my father's wishes, something that my stepmother felt strongly about, yet still act in a way that we could all feel good about. In deference to my feelings, our first plan was to take Dad's remains to the river, bury his ashes there and plant a tree as a memorial. There were obvious problems with that, because to do it legally we needed permission just to plant the tree, let alone to bury ashes there. The area that would have meant the most is state-owned property, and there are carefully plotted-out plans for things like tree planting. The supervisor with whom I spoke was kind, but he could not allow us to upset that plan. Plus, I consulted a deacon about conducting a service, and he told us we could do as we'd planned, as long as we marked the site in some way.

"It's part of honoring the sacredness of the body," Deacon Tony Ternes said. "You don't want somebody to come along later and dig the ashes up or disturb them in ways you didn't anticipate." Getting permission to plant the tree was tough. Getting permission to plant a tree with a burial plaque proved impossible. We were back to the scattering idea.

Fortunately, my brother and I were not interested in squabbling over it. We have always been good friends, and the best way we could honor our father was to make sure we kept that relationship intact. So while he may not have shared all of my Catholic views, he recognized that they were important to me, and he was willing to come up with a solution that would satisfy all.

Sadly, many families suffer fractured relationships that break completely when somebody dies. "Most families experience some levels of dysfunction at stressful times, and funerals are usually stressful," Becker says. "Blended families complicate things even more. People tend to slip back into the roles they occupied from the beginning. This is not the time to work out family problems."

Schumacher says the saddest times in his ministry are when families end the process not talking to each other. Those are wounds that he says sometimes are never healed.

"Suppose there are three children," he says. "The daughter stays home and lives near her aging mother, and she's taken care of her and has had daily interaction with her. The sons live their busy lives elsewhere, though they visit on occasion. They don't see the deterioration in Mom that the daughter sees; the pain involved, the loss of everyday pleasures. So she can accept it when Mom asks for a 'Do Not Resuscitate' order. The daughter's proximity to her dying mother has allowed her to begin to accept her impending death. But the sons, feeling guilty for going away and for not being as attentive as they should have been, come storming in demanding that the daughter do everything possible. 'You can't just let her die!' they'll say. In trying to work out their guilt, they may try to pull rank on the person who's been there all along, or even accuse her of incompetent care. This creates chaos in an atmosphere that was formerly peaceful."

Gayton sees this over and over again, too, played out in the emergency room as the family is gathered around a dying loved one. "It's almost always the family member who lives far away who says [to] do everything possible to save them," he says. He has watched hundreds of people die, and he says that when he has a chance to talk with the patient, he can usually get a good idea of what they do or don't want.

"They get a look in their eye when they're dying," he says. "I can't describe it, but I know it when I see it. People know when they are approaching death." But the struggle often happens when family members haven't yet accepted it. Gayton says he may tell a patient that he or she can be kept alive on machines that will breathe for them, or help their organs to function, but they need to realize that their chances of coming off of those machines and going back to any kind of normal life are very small. At that point, he says, they usually agree that they don't want extraordinary measures. It can be harder to tell the family, and they don't always agree. Again, he says, "you have to explain what life will be like. In the end they may not recognize family, they're wearing diapers, they can't feed themselves and they're sick, so they feel awful. Once families understand that, they're less inclined to say they want everything done." It's a conversation that he's had to have many times.

He says it's also a benefit, working at a Catholic hospital, that within minutes of being called, a clergy person is there. "What they say about people finding faith at the end," he says. "It's pretty true."

Richter tells a story of being called to the bedside of a man who was very sick, although his family felt that he was getting better. Still, they thought he would benefit from being anointed. The man's family was gathered around him as the prayers were said, and then Richter asked the family if he could have a few minutes alone with the man. After they left the room, he asked the man if he had anything private that he wanted to share, and the man did. He told Richter that he knew he was dying, but his family didn't realize it or hadn't accepted it. The two worked out together what he would say to his wife and children to make his passing easier for them, and then Richter stood by while they had that difficult conversation.

Gayton says he sees end-of-life suffering every day, and it has strengthened his faith. When he was younger, he says, he had a natural fear of death, but now that he's older, he says, "If I die tomorrow, I'm fine with it. I know my family will be taken care of. I don't fear there are worse things to come. Is it better? I don't know, but I think so, and I'm not afraid." Plus, he says, "I see people who have survived when I've thought there's no way in the world they can survive this. I do think there are miracles; I do." But most of the time, particularly when it concerns the elderly, the miracle might take on a different form: a person who wakes up from a coma to say a final goodbye, for instance, or bringing families together when it seemed certain that death would push them further apart.

Gayton says the person who lives closest very often has the power of attorney and will feel enormous pressure in the decision making. "What I tell them is that they aren't making the decision to let the patient die," he says. "Nature is making the decision. It's natural to die. It's unnatural to be kept alive on machines." But when the family members don't agree with that final decision, guilt can be magnified.

Sadder still are the fights that happen over the disbursement of possessions. "The last gathering is often the funeral, and then these people never talk to each other again," says Schumacher. "I've had to sit families on opposite sides of the church and I've had siblings 'boycott' their parents' funerals; it can get that bad. These funerals sadden me. The parents have worked hard all their lives, provided well and passed on an abundance of wealth. And the result? Their children become enemies."

He stresses the importance of talking about these issues long before death comes. Pre-plan for your final illness and death and for your funeral. Better yet, he says, pay for it. Somebody has to pay for it, and it can create a lot of tension in families if there are no plans in place. Becker agrees. In fact, he says wise people choose neutral parties to guide the funeral process, people who don't have a vested interest.

My brother and I finally decided to bury my father's ashes at the North Dakota Veterans Cemetery. When he looked at the location, my brother realized that this was really just steps away from where he and my father used to fish. And a military burial was an honor that he'd earned. So, two months after his death, my brother made the trek across the country to retrieve Dad's ashes from our stepmother. With her blessing, he and his family brought them to the cemetery, where Dad was buried with full military honors. Additionally, it gave me a chance to contact the church and have a presider at the service to say a few words and offer blessings on my father and on our family. It was a very moving ceremony, one I would not have missed, and I'm sure my father would not have disapproved.

Chapter 10

What About Purgatory?

"Christ strode through the gate of our final loneliness, that in his Passion he went down into the abyss of our abandonment. Where no voice can reach us any longer, there is he." Cardinal Josef Ratzinger, *Introduction to Christianity*.

If only: That's what many of us go through our lives saying to ourselves. "If only I had done this instead of that," and then we beat ourselves up over the choices we've made. I once knew a man who, by all accounts, lived a fine life, helped his friends and neighbors, honored God and did his work with integrity. But somewhere in his past he committed some deed that he considered to be unforgivable. Because of this, he was certain that he had not earned Heaven, and so he greatly feared death. He hung onto life long past the time when most people would have given up. His last years were a misery, and yet he feared eternal punishment so much that he clung to life.

For Christians, this fear that we've committed an unpardonable sin should be erased because Jesus died for us. He forgave Peter for denying Him, He forgave the Apostles for running away, He even forgave those who crucified Him while He was hanging from a cross, because He is God, and God is love. So it's inconceivable that He would not have forgiven this man for the wrong he had committed.

Catholics have the sacrament of reconciliation to fall back on, which can bring great comfort. Not everybody takes advantage of it, however, and sometimes even when we do, we find it difficult to forgive ourselves. And yet, how many of us get through life without a single regret? Even the saints made errors. They were as human as we are. So what happens, then, when we die if we have areas of our life that we view with shame? The *Catechism of the Catholic Church* says you may enter into purgatory as you await purification and Heaven, as all things in Heaven are pure. It makes sense that you'd want to be able to leave all those past sins and regrets behind you when you enter paradise. The trouble with the whole idea is that it's been taught to us in a frightening way. We hear about being purified by fire, the pain of Purgatory, and so on. It adds to our fear of death.

It's also been controversial. Many believe that the whole idea got its start during the Middle Ages as a way for the church to make money by selling indulgences – a sort of "Get Out Of Jail Free" card that one could buy. Because the church is made up of people and people are imperfect, there were undoubtedly people through the ages who took advantage, profiting from the fears of others.

But the idea of a place between this world and perfect happiness in Heaven is certainly not a Catholics-only concept. The Jews prayed for the dead long before the establishment of Christianity. If we all died and went straight to Heaven, why would there be a need for that? People in Heaven don't need our prayers. This time in between is mentioned in scripture in various places, even in the ancient texts. And it's mentioned in the New Testament.

Buddhists believe that there is an intermediate space between this world and the next called the bardo where the consciousness goes to wait. Tibetan Buddhist teacher Rinpoche Thupten Gyaltsen Dorje says there are four major bardos: the bardo of life, the bardo of dreams, the bardo of death and the bardo of becoming, but knowing that they exist doesn't necessarily bring comfort. "We all fear death," he says. People who practice meditation in the Buddhist tradition can meditate on the bardo, preparing themselves and thus relieving some of that fear. "Those who make a graceful exit know how to embrace death," Dorje says. "In preparing to die, one is preparing for the next life." And in the Muslim tradition, when people die they must wait to be judged in a place called Al-Barzakh, a kind of barrier between the physical and spiritual worlds, where they await resurrection and Judgment Day. Those who have lived a good life will go to different levels of Heaven. Those who don't will go to different levels of Hell. These are very elementary explanations for complicated beliefs, and each is different, but they are also similar in that they involve waiting with the hope of moving on to a better existence.

Monsignor Gene Lindemann is a Catholic pastor. He acknowledges that people of different faiths approach death in different ways, but he believes that there is a certain commonality to it as well. "Every faith has something beyond this life," he says. "God wires us to be united with Him, and however we interpret that, from whatever perspective, our deepest yearning is for that unity."

Lindemann assumes that he'll go to purgatory. "I think there's a need to allow the fire of God's love to purify us," he says. But he says purgatory isn't God punishing us. "The punishment is the delay in being able to experience the totality of God's love. That's what Heaven is; the totality of God's love. There are parts of me that haven't allowed God's love totally into my life. I still do things that are contrary to God's love." Thus, he believes that there is a need for purgatory. But he says there's no need to fear it.

Jesus, Son of David, have pity on me! - Mark 10:47

Christians have real evidence of how God treats sinners. In the New Testament, when Jesus is confronted with a sinner, what is His reaction? Does He throw rocks at her, or does He instead prevent others from doing so? Does He suggest that sinners be tossed into the fire? Does He turn His face away from them because their sins made them ugly? No. Jesus met them with love, not giving them a pass on their behavior, but gathering them in, despite their shortcomings. Plus, there's this: *For God so loved the world that He gave His only begotten son, that whoever believes in Him shall not perish but have eternal life.* (John 3:16) If that isn't evidence enough, consider your own behavior. What would your children have to do in order for you to toss them into a burning pit? Can you even imagine such a thing? God is our father. He does not consign us to the fires of Hell. Catholic tradition says that if we end up in a place far from Him, in a place of suffering, it's because we turned our face away from Him, not the other way around.

Thus He made atonement for the dead that they might be freed from this sin - 2 Maccabees 12:46

Catholic tradition also has us pray for the souls in purgatory. The human mind is trained to think in a linear fashion, so we probably imagine that every prayer takes, say, an hour off of somebody's time there. But really, because God is not bound by time and space, one has to wonder whether there is "time" in the afterlife. I believe our prayers can and do help those who have gone before us. Our sacred writings tell us this. But because time doesn't necessarily exist for God and for eternity, how do we know how long purgatory takes? Is it an instant of understanding at the moment of death? Who knows? But part of trusting in God is trusting that He will take care of us if we simply allow Him to do so, now and at the moment of death. We simply need to want that, to want Him.

Padre Pio was one of the church's great saints who lived in the modern era. He was given the gift of seeing through to a person's soul, and he believed in God's desire to care for us even though we don't deserve it. He said: "I believe that not a great number of souls go to Hell. God loves us so much. He formed us at His image. God loves us beyond understanding. And it is my belief that when we have passed from the consciousness of the world, when we appear to be dead, God, before He judges us, will give us a chance to see and understand what sin really is. And if we understand it properly, how could we fail to repent?"

My aim is not to try to prove or disprove purgatory as an actual place. Greater minds than mine have wrestled with the question, and the truth is that only those who die can know if it exists and what it is like. Rather, my aim is to take away the fear of it, because

I believe in the total mercy of God. He will assist you in whatever way is necessary to draw you to Him, no matter what your religious beliefs.

So that leaves the question, does *anybody* go to Hell? "We leave that in the hands of God," says Lindemann. "We always have to believe in the mercy of God, but there's always a call to conversion. Even though I don't deserve it, He offers it to me. But you need to receive it. God is merciful, but what do I do with that? Does it change me? God doesn't condemn you," he adds, "but you can condemn yourself."

Becker also believes that Hell is a choice. "People can choose to separate themselves from God, and God will let us do that for eternity, but He doesn't consign us to it," he says. "Theologians tell us very few people choose to do that. It's the ultimate sin – that you choose to separate yourself from God forever."

Our scripture tells us that Jesus will chase us, even into Hell. We pray this in our Apostle's Creed. "He descended into Hell," or in some translations, "He descended to the dead." Catholic theology teaches that this is God conquering death. In the words of St. John Chrysostum, "He that was taken by death has annihilated it! He descended into Hades and took Hades captive!"

St. Thomas Aquinas didn't deny the existence of Hell, but rather, offered words of comfort to those struggling with sin and disillusionment. "No matter how much one is afflicted, one ought always hope in the assistance of God and have trust in Him. There is nothing so serious as to be in the underworld. If, therefore, Christ delivered those who were in the underworld, what great confidence ought every friend of God have that he will be delivered from all his troubles!"

In the end, it comes down to trust. Do you trust that God can make whatever change in you is necessary so that you can leave all your baggage behind and join Him? Because all through history, God's message has been the same: "I love you. Do you love me? Do you trust me enough to hand your life over to me, or do you hang on to your own stubborn will and desires?"

"That's original sin, isn't it?" says Lindemann. "And it's still with us today."

Chapter 11

When the End Finally Comes

Jesus Christ, having entered the sanctuary of Heaven once and for all, intercedes constantly for us as the mediator who assures us of the permanent outpouring of the Holy Spirit – Catechism of the Catholic Church

The last outing I had with my father was to the grocery store. It was his wife's birthday and the two of them had a tradition. He always bought her a German chocolate cake and a single red rose. The store we visited was huge, with the staples laid out along the edges. The first thing Dad did was grab a cart because then he could walk without assistance and not lose his balance. He could look like everybody else. I realized how important this was to him when my brother stepped forward to assist him in getting out of the car and he said, "You're treating me like an old man." My brother, in his teasing fashion, answered, "I've got news for you, Dad. You *are* an old man." But even so, we grabbed a grocery cart for him to hold on to and left him to it.

Dad was heading to the bakery, a man with a mission, and he told us it might take a few minutes, so my brother and I wandered off in different directions, each to our own shopping. Then I went to the bakery and Dad wasn't there. Worse, they hadn't seen him. I began marching up and down the aisles looking for him. My brother finally found him on the opposite end of the store. He'd become confused and then lost. He was baffled and upset because he'd been in that store a thousand times. On the way to the florist to pick up the flower he'd ordered, he admitted to me that this wasn't the first time he'd gotten lost on home turf.

Again, because I lived far away, and because my dad couldn't travel, I typically saw him only once or twice a year, so when I saw him standing in his doorway during this last visit, I was shocked at how tiny he had become. He'd always been a robust man, not terribly tall, but muscular, with a barrel chest and broad shoulders. Now he was gaunt. He'd told me during our weekly phone conversations that he didn't have much of an appetite these days and that he'd been losing weight. Still, it was a surprise to see that he'd meant it. He truly was a mere shadow of the man I'd known. But his eyes were clear. He was able to play cards the way we always had during our visits. His sense of humor was intact. It wasn't until that trip to the grocery store that I realized he really was nearing the end of his life. That's when it finally sank in.

When I was a small child, it was mainly my mother who cared for me and my brother. Dad was gone a lot. But when he was home, he was present to us. He played with us. We spent hours around the kitchen table playing games like Crazy 8s or Hearts or Monopoly. In those years he was always good for a game of catch in the back yard, and he didn't give me any special treatment, either. I never did learn to throw well, but he never gave up on me, even when it was clear that I would always throw like a girl. I could run fast, and I could hit the ball, and he let me know that those qualities were good enough. My brother was his hunting and fishing buddy. They spent hours together walking through stubble fields flushing out pheasants or sitting in boats waiting for the walleyes to bite. I daresay they knew each other better than I knew either of them. But for me he was like a positive mirror, reflecting back all my best qualities. I knew I'd done well when Dad was impressed, and pleasing him was paramount while I was growing up. I believe that he affected others that way as well, including his stepchildren and grandchildren. He held us to a higher standard, and we wanted to reach that goal because he expected it. As an adult, I often looked to him when I had troubles. He would always listen and while he didn't always have the answers, he always left me with the feeling that everything would be all right.

When a person dies, we tend to paint them as perfect. The man with feet of clay suddenly becomes a saint during his eulogy. Dad was far from perfect. He could be cranky. He loved the individual, but he could be very hard on people he didn't know, people with whom he disagreed or people who were different from him. Yet he was charm itself when meeting someone for the first time, which is what made him such a good salesman. People liked him and he had lifelong friends. He never knew how to handle money, so he was almost always broke. But when he loved, he loved completely.

When my brother and I arrived at the hospital that final time, Dad was on a ventilator and was heavily sedated. He gave no indication that he knew we were there. We talked to him in hushed voices, the way people do around the extremely ill. We let him know that we had come, then kissed him goodnight and went home to sleep. In the morning, we gathered again around his hospital bed in the ICU and waited for the family meeting that had been scheduled for that day. The hospitalist came into the room and told us that Dad would not improve, that he could not survive without the machines, and he matter-of-factly recommended that we shut them off. Karen did not want to be the one to make the decision, but really, there was no need to debate it. It was clear that Dad was dying. We assembled in the hallway and then each of us went back into his glass cubicle for a private moment with him. I told him that he'd been a good father to me, that I didn't want him to be afraid, and then I prayed with him. We all cried. His heart doctor came in then and said words that had real impact.

"Thank you for being here," he said. "Had I been in the ER when they brought your father in, I would not have let them put him on these machines. I know he wouldn't want this. He's my friend. It's time he goes to be with God."

Perhaps it was good that the doctor had not been there. I believe it was God in His mercy who intervened, possibly at my father's request. Those two days gave us time to be at his bedside, not only to say goodbye, but to be there as support for his wife, whom he had dearly loved for nearly 25 years. She left the room when the tubes and monitors were removed and the machines were turned off. She apologized to us, saying, "I have watched him die for a year. I can't be in here when it really happens." Then she took a seat in the hallway and began to quietly fall apart. She shook from head to toe. I didn't see tears so much as an agony of spirit. She was torn between her fear and her desire to be there for him at the end. Her daughter and a family friend sat with her outside the room, wrapping her in blankets and talking to her, doing their best to distract her, with little success.

When the machines were quiet, we all stood around barely breathing, watching his chest rise and fall. The thing was, though, he didn't die. Having never been at a death bed before, I expected it to happen quickly, the way it does in movies, but it didn't. He appeared to be breathing normally on his own and looked for all the world as if he were sleeping. He even began to gently snore, a sound that I'd heard from him all my life. It was comforting in a way. As the hours ticked by, we started taking turns sitting with Karen in the hallway, sitting with Dad in his room. Sandwiches were brought in, which at first we felt uncomfortable eating, but eventually we did as the hours ticked by.

We heard a lot of commotion at one point, and a nurse came in to tell us there'd been a serious accident and they needed the ICU bed that Dad was occupying. Incredibly, they were going to move him, and us. At first I greeted this news with consternation, but as we all settled into a family "comfort" room on a different floor, something amazing began to happen. The scariness of the situation dissipated. Karen finally came into the room and sat with us, and with Dad. Life started going on around him as he lay sleeping. We talked and laughed; it was almost as if we were in Dad's living room at a family get-together. We told stories about him and shared details of our lives in different cities.

It was a long and, in some ways, a good day. As evening approached, we decided that we had to try to get Karen to eat something, so we talked about bringing in dinner. That's when Karen said, "I'm just so tired. I think I need to go home. I don't want to leave but I need to lie down." The words were no sooner out of her mouth than Dad's breathing changed, each breath further apart than the last. As we realized he was really leaving us, Karen got up from her chair and walked to his side. She told him that she loved him, she kissed him and asked him to save a place for her when her time came. And then his breathing stopped altogether. At that moment, a nurse we had not seen up to that point came in and offered support. Though he wasn't breathing, his pulse remained, and she told us in a quiet voice, "He can still hear you." We all told him again that we loved him, that it was okay to go, and we held his hands.

Is there an actual moment of death? Or is it like conception, more of a process? When does the spirit leave the body? One could argue that because my father never woke up, he was not really there at the end. You could say that it was merely coincidence, his last breaths coming at the moment when Karen had finally had all she could take. But I believe otherwise. As Ehli said, there are no coincidences in death.

Having had time to reflect, I believe that Dad lingered long enough for Karen to find the courage to say goodbye. I believe the send-off that he had, with all of us there in his room, not happy exactly, but full of life, was his own form of caretaking. This was his final gift to us, and I believe it was of his choosing. So no, he wasn't perfect. But his last act on earth was one of love.

God reads our hearts and knows who we are in those final moments. Whatever happens, He does whatever He can to draw us to Himself as only a father can.

"We need to cling to Christ," says Richter. "We need to believe that at the moment of death, God wants His children to feel comfort, hope, strength and faith. Those are from Him. A good death is a heart that never succumbs to the mean thoughts, feelings and desires that say 'Maybe God doesn't care.'"

Consider again the death of a child, who fights until the end, but then gives up the struggle, relaxes and lets go. God builds into us the will to live, but at the end we need to become like children, full of that trust that brings us peace. Pray for that.

Psalm 23

The Lord is my shepherd; I shall not want.

In verdant pastures he gives me repose;

Beside restful waters he leads me; he refreshes my soul.

He guides me in right paths for his name's sake.

Even though I walk in the dark valley I fear no evil; for you are at my side with your rod and your staff that give me courage.

You spread the table before me in the light of my foes;

You anoint my head with oil; my cup overflows.

Only goodness and kindness follow me all the days of my life;

And I shall dwell in the house of the Lord for years to come.

ABOUT THE AUTHOR

Monica Hannan is an Emmy-award-winning broadcast journalist and author of the *The Dream Maker*. She also co-authored *Dakota Daytrips* and *More Dakota Daytrips*.

Author Photograph by Deborah Kates